# TRIATHLON: THE INEPT IRONMAN

RYAN A. BREWER

edited by Kim Miller

For Kelli, Dustin, Dave, Gary, Wanda, Barbara, Addison, and Lauren. Thank you for all your support, patience, motivation, and love. You are only as good as the people who surround you.

# Introduction

When I decided to give the Ironman a shot, I searched for hours on Netflix, Hulu, YouTube, Facebook, and every streaming service I could find for the key word "triathlon." Then I explored the high heavens for interesting books and audio. I read motivating stories about guys literally dying—then coming back to life—to complete an Ironman. I listened to stories of people who were addicted to hard drugs and miraculously righted the ship to do the same. I witnessed a military veteran with a leg amputated below the knee race, and not slowly might I add. I also watched a father swim with his disabled son in a raft, bike with him on a trailer, and push him on a cart for 140.6 miles. I watched low budget films tell fun stories, albeit with terrible acting, about how triathlon is an amazing sport which could transform your life. The biggest genre I found was a bunch of guys under forty documenting their first triathlon experience through YouTube and doing product reviews while telling you the perfect way to train.

Although I really enjoyed a lot of these films, audiobooks, and stories, none of them were directed specifically towards me and my internal motivations.

The more I searched, the more I realized that no one—and I mean no one—has written a book about a normal dude (or dudette) with a normal job and a normal family who decided to complete an Ironman.

If you watch any Ironman World Championships telecast, they show clips of unbelievable stories and impossible recoveries. They focus on athletes who overcame unimaginable circumstances. They pull at your heart strings and motivate you. They cover the professionals, because that's what we really want to see, but they rarely follow the majority of the age group athletes in the race.

And in all honesty, the average participant is boring to follow for fifteen hours.

They never show the average, tough-as-nails, forty-year-old working his tail off to do something out of this world, despite the daily grind back home. I use "average" rather loosely here. Afterall, anyone training for an Ironman probably has a screw loose.

This is me: I'm forty years old and serve as an Air Force Reserve pilot. I have a beautiful wife and two amazing daughters. My mom and dad are a huge part of my life. I have a support team of friends who are always ready to go exercise or party, whenever the mood strikes. I like pizza…I mean *really* like pizza…to the point where I ate half a large extra pepperoni and cheese before my first and only Ironman, but that's a story you'll hear later. I drink bud light and sweet tea vodka. I eat McDonald's quarter-pounders and Popeye's spicy chicken sandwiches. I have a spare tire around my mid-section that embarrasses me every morning when I look in the mirror.

I don't enjoy swimming, biking, or running. I'd rather sit in my comfy chair and watch Atlanta sports from seven to eleven every night . . . exactly like I'm doing right now. I stay up late. I can't stand early morning workouts. I'm lazy most of the time. I've never had a near death experience or a problem with drugs or alcohol. I've never even had a serious injury or completed a mind-blowing feat. Now that I think of it, I'm kind of boring!

With that said, I've got a story and it's a pretty good one. This is a story of family and friends. A story of how motivation kicked me in gear when I thought my competitive sporting days were long over. A story of how I found courage to train when dark days came my way. A story of emotions and pains I never knew existed. A story of hoping my personal experience will be a life lesson that benefits my kids one day. A story that shows, in life, regrets are often simply missed opportunities that open gateways to where you find yourself today.

Finally, this is a story with a happy ending.

I invite you to journey with me—a normal dude who is fat, lazy, and kind of boring, but who happens to be an Ironman—sweet-ass tattoo and all! I hope my story stimulates your emotions and desires. I hope you take the next step and chase a lifelong goal. I hope you breakdown and spend $1,000 to do an Ironman or finally get off the couch and start moving. I hope you realize, even though you might be an average person, you are capable of doing something very few have done before.

Let's take a journey together . . . as average, normal folks.

# The Clock Strikes Midnight in Lake Placid, New York

At 10 p.m. on July 31, 2019, I huddled over my laptop in bed with my wife, watching the Ironman Lake Placid finish line on Facebook Live. We had spent the day in Birmingham, Alabama, shopping and eating all day. Throughout the day, I would check my Ironman Tracker app to see how Dave was doing.

Dave had started the race at 6:30 a.m. and was reaching the seventeen-hour cut-off-to-finish with only six miles to go. He'd swum 2.4 miles in freezing New York water. He'd biked 112 miles in one of the most treacherous, mountainous, courses in North America. He'd run 20 of the 26.2 miles of the marathon. The live feed featured music blaring and fans cheering. Mike Reilly, the voice of Ironman, pumped up the crowd. His unmistakable voice ensured spectators and online watchers were having the time of their life.

My wife had a nervous intensity about her. "Dave is going to finish," I assured her. Everything was going great.

Dave is my father-in-law. The guy is crazy, but I love him. Here he was, competing in Lake Placid at age sixty-four, in his first ever Ironman—and checking off one more bucket list item. Through the years he'd completed many triathlons. In fact, he'd finished the Escape from Alcatraz Triathlon five times.

Dave is an athlete, plain and simple. He's a tough-as-nails, no-nonsense guy who appreciates hard work, determination, old school chivalry, and respect. All six feet and 185 pounds of him is built for triathlon. He played high school football in the 1970s . . . at the "heavy" weight of 175 pounds, a far cry from the behemoths we see today. He then played Rugby at

Auburn University. Moreover, he has a smoking hot daughter, that I happened to woo at a keg party, while home on break from college.

Did I mention he is a little bit nuts? Dave has been running, biking, and swimming since before he could crawl. If you walk behind him, you might think you've found yourself in an old John Wayne Western. He's been training so hard for so long that his legs bow like someone who rides horses all day. His knees hurt all the time so he uses a bionic brace to get that last mile out of his workouts. Despite his aging knees and faltering body, Dave only has one gear . . . and that gear is GO! Damn the torpedoes, full speed ahead! He quoted to me on a run one day, "I'll get new knees when these old ones fall off!"

I started working out and running with Dave shortly after marrying his daughter. He and I would wake up at the God-awful hour of 4:45 a.m. and drive to

Kennesaw Mountain in Marietta, Georgia. We would meet up with his high school friends and run the trails. His friends, the Doctor and the Accountant, called him Coach. They would banter back and forth about college football and excavate stories from back in the day. They would constantly poke fun at each other. They had tall tales for every thing and every place on the mountain trail. They had been running together for twenty years and it never got old. They would run different sections each week. They knew every root, stump, and rock. The coolest part was they never complained and they never stopped. Even if one person couldn't make it, the remaining soldiers would send a text at 4:45 a.m. to shame them for not showing up. It was comradery. It was friendship in its purest form. It was an escape from the daily grind. And it was *living*!

    They welcomed me with open arms. They slowed down while my hangover persisted from the night before. My favorite part was the stories and explanations of the trail. They had Sasquatch Flats, where they swear the mysterious creature appeared through dense fog. They had Wake-Up, three steep inclines that started one portion of the trail. The Three Sisters were massive climbs that killed your quads halfway into the run. Finally, Bamboo Salad, a section of 40-foot bamboo trees right in the middle of towering pines. I would settle in at their pace and listen to the stories while enjoying their company. A three-hour, ten-to-fourteen-mile jaunt would seem like only minutes when running with these guys.

Another thing, I was bonding with Dave. We both enjoyed the opportunity to be men. We ran, talked about crude and fun things, farted, and cussed. We discarded normal pleasantries that you deal with when in the company of in-laws.

This became our thing. Every time I drove into Atlanta to visit, I'd make sure I had the right clothing to run the trails. Sometimes it was jackets, gloves, and hoodies. Other times, it was ranger panties (short flimsy shorts) and tank tops. One thing was for sure, I rarely declined. Every chance presented to me, I'd go run with Dave. During these runs I started to ask him about his triathlons and the necessary training. He was my father-in-law, but he became my friend and training partner.

The online tracker suddenly stopped. The icon of Dave on my phone was *not* updating! He had passed mile twenty of the marathon with over two hours left to finish, then…NOTHING.

My wife said "Crap!" under her breath.

My heart sank.

She looked at me and said, "I'm worried that he is not okay. I mean, seriously not okay."

She'd watched her dad hobble on bad knees for years. She never particularly liked the idea of him completing an Ironman. Her worst fears were rising to the surface.

Dave's tracker wasn't moving, but the clock was still ticking.

We sat, waiting in bed, as midnight on the East Coast approached. We begged the app to update as we willed him on from hundreds of miles away. We wanted to watch him crawl across the finish line. We wanted him to complete his lifelong dream and hear Mike Reilly scream into the microphone, "Dave, YOU ARE AN IRONMAN!"

The phone rang right on cue. It was Barbara, Kelli's mom and Dave's wife. "Kelli, your dad had to pull out of the race. He is okay, but something happened to his leg. He said he needed to pull out before it became permanently damaged. He is heading back to the hotel room and he will call you later, but he is okay."

Kelli hung up the phone. "He didn't make it."

Her emotion was relief at first. Her dad didn't kill himself trying to complete one of the hardest competitions on the planet. Then her emotion turned to sorrow as reality set in. Her dad's bucket list item would remain unchecked on this fateful night.

My heart ached for Dave. I heard the stories of him at Alcatraz. The story of him being lifted out of the freezing San Francisco Bay water by the Loch Ness monster. I heard the stories of his long runs and countless hours of training in the pool leading up to this race. I felt horrible for him. I kept thinking over and over in my head, six miles, six measly miles!

"This can't be it," I said.

Then reality set in and I had an epiphany. I was proud of Dave. He placed his family and loved ones over his goals and ambitions. He sacrificed living out a dream to ensure he could enjoy time with my daughters. He made the right choice, and I applauded him for that . . . but six stinking miles! That is the cruelest joke I've ever seen pulled on anyone. I couldn't believe it. I started to think, what if? What if I had been there? Could I have made a difference? Could I have kept his mind busy with conversation on the run and kept his mind off the pain? Could I have fireman carried his ass the last six miles? Why wasn't I there to help him? Why couldn't I have been there for him like he was for me? He was always pushing me to get up every morning at 5 a.m. to better myself, hangover be damned! What if?

On that night, I made a decision that I wouldn't tell anyone for several months.

I was going to do an Ironman.

Not for me, but for Dave. And I didn't care if I died trying.

Moreover, I was going to try and get him to do it with me, even if it did completely destroy his knee. He'd forgive me if he never walked again…maybe. Heck, he'd have a great Ironman story that would probably get televised at the World Championships! Barbara and Kelli might send me packing from the family, but in the end, watching Dave's triumphant face at the end of a completed Ironman would be worth it.

We were going to do this whether he liked it or not. I owed it to him.

Sure, my college wrestling days were a speck in the rearview mirror, and I could lose a few pounds.

Plus, the best time to get in shape is always now. How hard could it be?

That, my friends, was the dumbest thought I've had in over twenty years.

But it was my first step on this crazy road to Ironman.

# The Gerbil and the Giraffe

Have you ever watched a professional runner—their grace, the length of their stride, their lack of movement from the waist up? They effortlessly glide over the pavement and breathing comes naturally.

Well, that's not me!

That's my best friend and daily training partner, Dustin.

Have you ever seen a scared chicken run? Wings spread wide, head bobbing back and forth, wheezing and crowing.

Well, that's me.

Yeah, my form is more like Sylvester Stallone's in *Rocky* when he's chasing chickens around the coup. In high school, my wrestling coach said I looked like a deranged goat on the side of the road. I was all elbows and knees flying here and there, stomping on the ground like I wanted to punish the pavement. I'm sure it was amusing to witness, but in my head, I was Usain Bolt in the 100-meter dash. I was graceful and smooth—straight-hauling ass! That is, until I started running with Dustin and paying attention to my pace and form. At that point, I realized something mind-bending. At five foot, eight inches and kind of tubby, I was not a good runner and had to work hard to put in the miles. Next to Dustin, I looked like a gerbil running with a giraffe, taking at least ten short choppy steps for every five of his long, graceful strides.

Dustin was a triathlete. He grew up in Southern California and has a "surfer dude" attitude and body—tall and lean, not an ounce of fat on him. He ate clean, because apparently that's what people from California do. We both went to the Air Force Academy, where he was captain of the triathlon team. Although only 4,000 students attend the Academy, we didn't know each other back then. We met when his wife and kids moved next door in temporary housing at Columbus Air Force Base in 2017. He was still traveling to Texas for training, and I was waiting on my house to be finished.

As we started hanging out, we realized not only did we both graduate in the class of 2003, we also married Southern peaches from Georgia. The bond was instant! Dustin is one of those guys who, when you meet him, you feel like you've known him forever. He is easy to talk to, fun to be around, and grounded morally. He's a hard worker, but he didn't have the greatest childhood. Despite all the crazy things going on around him, he came out on top. He enlisted in the Air Force and became a JTAC (Joint Terminal Attack Controller), the hardened soldiers who call in airstrikes from fighters and bombers. He was selected to attend the United States Air Force Academy shortly afterwards and became a pilot. I could write an entire book based on his story, but you'll get plenty of Dustin in due time.

Dustin and I started running together shortly after we met. Nothing crazy, just a few miles when we had a break from flying. He would slow down to a crawl for me, and we would chat about life, religion, and being dads. Over the first year together we built an amazing bond during our runs. I would tell him about all of my accomplishments from high school wrestling, what my wife calls my glory days. He would tell me about his triathlons and races throughout college and beyond. When Dave started training for his Ironman, Dustin told me he'd completed an Ironman 70.3 shortly after college. He said it was the hardest thing he had ever done. As if a half-Ironman wasn't enough for one day, he drove five hours home to move into a new house that same afternoon! Have I told you he is a little crazy too? You'll start to notice an interesting trend with craziness and triathlons if you haven't picked up on it yet. Anyways, we started talking about maybe getting into a few road races and a few triathlons.

# Ready, Set, Go!

In February 2018, we ran the Columbus Pilgrimage 5K—a scenic run through a quaint town in Mississippi. Dustin finished the race basically before I passed the half-mile point, but you better believe he was running with me and pushing me the last 300 feet to the finish line.

The next month we ran the Tuscaloosa Half Marathon. Dustin and I checked into a hotel room the night before and got everything ready to go—our watches and headphones charging, our clothes laid out, and our numbers pinned to our shirts.

We woke up the next morning and headed to the starting line. I looked down at my watch and it was only half charged. When I put my headphones in, they immediately turned off from low battery. I plugged them into the lamp next to my bed the night before but didn't realize the plugs only worked when the lamp was turned on. I cursed loud enough for the thousand people around me to stare at me like I forgot my shorts. Then I surrendered to the fact that my second half-marathon ever was going to be without music. Yay for me!

I am not a purist runner or distance athlete. I like my music! It keeps me going when I get bored. Growing up in Atlanta in the '90s, my playlists are composed of Tu Pac, Biggie, OutKast, and other gangster rap groups, but I'm also an '80s fanatic. When I was around twenty, I realized that I knew every lyric to every '80s song ever made. It took me another five years to realize that I knew the songs because I would listen to them every day when driving in the back seat of my mom's car growing up. Needless to say, I do not enjoy listening to myself huff and puff and wheeze when I run. I prefer a beat and some good lyrics to keep me going. Dave, the purist, always gives me a hard time about this.

My second half-marathon and no damned music. This race was gonna suck!

On top of that, my giraffe friend, Dustin, told me he was going to take it easy and run with me, but he was jittery like a crack addict—visibly vibrating from race-day adrenaline.

That's when I knew the race was going to be the worst one yet.

The gun went off. Dustin and I jogged and stopped, then weaved and bobbed around the runners in front of us until the crowd thinned.

About one hundred yards in, Dustin looked and me and said, "Bro, I gotta go!"

I laughed and said, "Well, then GO!"

Boy, did he. He shot out like a cannon and turned the first corner, never to be seen again—that is, until the last 300 feet.

Dustin, like Dave, only has one speed and that speed is ludicrous. Heaven forbid someone be in front of him at a race. He will chase you down like a damn cheetah on the African Sahara and then brush your shoulder while yelling "ON YOUR LEFT" as he passes by. Luckily, I've never been in front of Dustin, so I've never been one of his victims. But I've seen some pretty fast, mean looking dudes get hunted down by him on the course, and it is very entertaining to watch.

My slow start and steady pace along with all the training had me feeling pretty dang good at mile ten when we hit the first big hill. I was able to plow through and pass a bunch of people.

I ended up finishing the half-marathon in two hours and five minutes. This was a respectable time for a free-range chicken.

At the 300-yard mark, Dustin ran along the fence.

My awesome wife and kids were cheering me at the finish line, just like every race. They are my support team and my fan club. They're always there, always cheering, and always smiling. They are the reason I love finish lines.

This time—without my headphones—I could actually hear them cheering because I wasn't listening to the Notorious B.I.G sing, "Ughhhh, baby baby!"

Isn't it funny how sometimes when you think nothing is going as planned, you find that it was probably meant to be. Sometimes you have to unplug, literally, to get the full experience. Had I not lost my music, I wouldn't have enjoyed Dustin screaming my name and my wife and children beaming with smiles and cheering me on so loudly.

The race that I thought was going to be my worst, ended up being one of my favorites.

# My First Triathlon

My first triathlon was with about fifty-five people at Columbus Air Force Base in May 2019. It consisted of a 300-yard snaking pool swim, a 17-mile bike ride, and a 3.1-mile run. This was a sprint triathlon and the perfect race to get my feet wet. I had an old Specialized, road bike, that I trained on. Dustin and I swam in the mornings before work and ran whenever we could. By race day, I felt in shape and Dustin, well . . . I don't think he's ever been out of shape.

Dustin started first in the pool. I started in the back with the other slow people so I wouldn't be passed in demoralizing fashion. By the time I got to the bike, I'm pretty sure Dustin was halfway back to the second transition. I hopped on my bike and took off. The swim felt good in the hot May heat of Mississippi. The bike ride was short enough that I wasn't worried about being drained before the upcoming run. I laid the hammer down on the bike. When I say laid the hammer down, I was doing a whopping seventeen miles an hour! If you know anything about biking, you'd know that this is the speed at which five-year-olds cruise around the neighborhood on their tricycles.

    I finished the bike, ate a Clif bar (which I later realized was a total waste of time), then sat down, put on my running shoes, stood, then took off. Different from the swim and bike, I actually ran a pretty good race. My pace of 7:45 per mile for the 5K was the fastest I'd ever run that distance. Out of the three disciplines, running was definitely my favorite, because it was the one I'd been doing since before high school. I grew up swimming in lakes, creeks, and ponds in Georgia. Not that I was fast or had good form, but swimming didn't bother me either. I honestly hated biking. I mean, capital HATED it, but it was a means of getting to the run. I was willing to put up with the miserable two-wheeled torture machine if it meant getting a medal in the end.

I got first in my age group!

You might be wondering what happened to Dustin.

He beat me in the race as expected. In fact, he finished first overall and got his own special award for being top finisher. And since he was the overall winner, he was no longer in my age group for awards. Thanks to his blazing speed, I slotted up from second to first in our age group.

Medal around my neck, the hook was in. I had found my new competitive sport. It was time to set the said hook and reel it in.

# Special "Dad" Moment

After that race, something special happened. Well, it started the day before. The base was supposed to have a kid's triathlon on Friday before the adult competition on Saturday. But that morning, right at race time, a huge storm moved through. They had to cancel the kids' portion. My youngest daughter Lauren had signed up for the race. Her poor little seven-year-old heart was broken. She had seen me running and biking around the neighborhood, and I had coaxed her into signing up. She wasn't extremely interested in triathlon per se, but she wanted to do something with her Daddy. She even trained a little bit. She would be on her twenty-inch pink bike with streamers pedaling at 120 revolutions per minute around the circle in our neighborhood. Next, she would break out in a full-on sprint, followed by long stretches of breathless walking around the same circle. Sadly, she didn't get the chance to officially race.

As they put a medal around my neck after the triathlon the next day, I could see a little sparkle in her eye. But I also noticed a little disappointment.

With my best fatherly instinct, I grabbed her. We went over to the pool, and I pulled out my watch and hit start. She jumped in and swam her little heart out across the twenty-five-yard pool. She hopped out and we ran together to our bikes. She got on, and we rode for about two miles down the road and back. The smile on her face was contagious and those streamers on her handlebars were flying like a fighter jet! Then she ran with me for a full mile.

As we rounded the corner to the finish line, the blow-up arch was still in place, along with all the athletes from the adult competition who were drinking beer and hanging out. Lauren burst through the finish line ahead of me, breathing harder than I could've ever imagined. Her older sister, Addison, who is the most loving and caring kid on the planet, took my medal and placed it around her neck and handed her a red Gatorade. Her favorite! Kelli hugged her neck. I picked her up and spun her around. Even all the adult triathletes were clapping and cheering for her. She was in pure bliss.

What a great moment. What a proud moment as a father. How funny is it, that a sport like this can bring so much pain and suffering one minute, yet amazing pride and elation the next. I tell my girls that hard work always pays off and "If it isn't hard, it probably isn't worth doing."

This was her moment!

I hope a long time from now, she will remember
that race and how it made her feel.

# Stepping Up Our Game

Shortly after the Air Force base triathlon, while basking in our old man glory, I told Dustin, "Well, I guess the next step is going to be an Olympic-distance triathlon. Let's look around and see what's available." Dustin looked at me but didn't say a word. He just grinned. He already had the next race planned and ready to go. It was as if he already knew my thoughts and exactly what I needed and wanted to do.

We got online and started scrolling. The Chattanooga Waterfront Triathlon was coming up in June. This triathlon would be more than the sprint distances I had completed. I was ready to take the next step. My parents live on the east side of Chattanooga. We not only had a free place to stay, but the kids could also visit with Nana and Pop.

Our training ramped up. We increased our running distances, swam in the mornings at the base swimming pool, and rode our bikes on the base's perimeter road over the weekends. We didn't have a set training schedule or a coach helping us along. We were simply excited and motivated, working out as much as two dudes who had full-time jobs, wives, and kids could. We hit the training hard all month and showed up at Chattanooga primed and ready to go.

Chattanooga is a beautiful city nestled in the Appalachian Mountains with iconic bridges that cross the Tennessee River as it winds through the northern part of the city. The triathlon included a 900-yard swim in the Tennessee River, a 26-mile bike that looped east over the hills, and a 6.2-mile run that started along the riverbank and then shifted south into some nice rolling hills.

Rolling hills is a nice way to say it. Living in the flat farmland of Mississippi, I wasn't sure what the hills were going to do to me, but I soon found out. Like most summer days in the South, it was hot as hell and the sun shone brightly. As I stood on the dock 900 yards from the transition area, I realized this was my first true triathlon. I wasn't on Columbus Air Force Base with its chlorinated pool, closed roads, and flat landscape. I put on my swim cap and fastened the goggles tight. My heart raced and I took in a deep breath.

The triathletes who surrounded me were all shapes and sizes. Some fat, some skinny, some tall and some short. I looked around and as my gaze fell on one guy, I thought, "Man, is that dude seriously gonna do this race?"

Sure enough, no matter the body type or gender, they just kept jumping in the water every five seconds, one after the other. As I stood watching, I realized firsthand that anyone can do anything they put their mind to. It doesn't matter what you look like on the outside, it's what you have on the inside that counts.

Still, all these shapes and sizes befuddled me. In my wrestling days, I saw guys so muscular they looked like they had walked straight out of the weight room. And I saw long, lanky guys who could twist you up like a pretzel. Very rarely, even among heavyweight wrestlers, did I see athletes with huge spare tires around their waist step onto the mat. Maybe that's because we were all in our late teens and early twenties, but who knows. Seeing this huge variance of people starting a triathlon was interesting and inspiring. All these people—despite their size, age, color, or political persuasion—were standing at that start line with a big smile on their face about to do something to make themselves better. This was just another reminder of why I loved the sport so much.

I hit the water. It was dark, I couldn't see anything around me, and I kept getting hit and kicked from all sides. I didn't freak out. I'd heard horror stories from Dave and Dustin about triathlon swims. Sometimes, in the first hundred yards or so, you can find people floating on their backs, looking up at the sky, searching for something, anything to calm their nerves and slow down their heart rates. Dave told me that the water was so cold in San Francisco for Alcatraz that his body literally went into shock the first five minutes. Luckily for me, even though I'm not a good swimmer, I'm comfortable in the water. As long as I know there are no sharks, I'm good! No JAWS had ventured this far upstream in the Tennessee River as far as I knew.

I swam, and I swam, and I swam.

I looked up, and I still hadn't passed the second bridge which was 300 yards from the water exit. I thought, "How long is this thing?"

Little did I know that I had been swimming a zigzag pattern the entire time. Later when I looked at my Garmin watch, it showed that I swam an additional 300 yards because I wasn't spotting the buoys correctly.

Finally, I finished the swim and hopped out of the water where my family awaited my arrival near the transition area.

Kelli asked, "How was it?"

I responded, "Really long!"

I hit transition and sped off on the bike. The bike course was interesting. Right off the bat, there were two big climbs of at least 300 feet. With bike handling skills that rivaled my girls when they were learning to ride without training wheels, I put my head down and pedaled as hard as I could. About ten minutes into the bike, I was pedaling super hard and still looking straight down, oblivious to the fact that I was drifting across the right lane.

At the very top of the first hill, I accidentally swerved hard left. My erratic movement startled a triathlete passing me. As he veered left to get out of my way, his front tire went straight into a gap in the concrete bridge.

All I heard was "Shiiiiiiiiiiiiiiiiiit!"

I glanced back to see his body flying over the handlebars.

I should have stopped to help him out. I should have made sure he was okay. All I did was look back quickly and say, "Are you okay?"

He nodded, so I continued on.

I now realize I totally ruined that guy's race, even though it was a complete accident.

Let's just say that karma is a bitch, and it came back for vengeance. I finally got over the hills and settled into a nice groove. Did I tell you I really hate biking? When I say settling in, I mean a whopping sixteen miles per hour.

I got comfortable and wasn't paying attention again, and BAM! I ran right over an orange construction cone marking the course. I'm not kidding.

My bike wobbled and thrashed, and I was too stupid to unclip from my pedals. I veered hard right and then hard left and somehow, by the grace of God, stayed upright. Talk about embarrassing. I must have looked like Pee Wee Herman out there riding on the course. "What a fool," I thought to myself. I determined to pay attention the rest of the way.

Cautiously, I continued . . . getting passed by every person on the course. Do you remember all of those "big" people I was talking about at the swim start line? All of those old people who I didn't think should be doing the race? Well, let's just say I ate a big ole chunk of humble pie around mile twelve. The only person I was able to pass was a guy on a mountain bike with no clip-in pedals.

By the time I made it back to the transition area, I was so glad to get off my bike. I hit the run course at a cool eight-minute, thirty-second pace. Unfortunately, the temperature had gotten up to eighty-nine degrees. I was not ready for what ensued.

Somehow, I totally forgot about the fourth discipline of triathlon: nutrition. I had a slice of orange and a mini-Clif bar prior to the race. On the bike I drank twenty-four ounces of water. When I hit the hill at mile two of the run, my quick pace slowed to a walk and then a dead stop. They had cold towels at the first water station, and I draped one over my head. I drank as much water as I could find. The aid station workers gave me funny looks. I was beet red and sweating profusely. I looked like Mad Max walking out of the desert in Thunderdome.

Because I'm not a quitter and because I'm too hardheaded to know what's good for me, I kept on.

Somehow, I made it to the last 300 yards.

Did you guess it? Dustin was waiting on me! He finished about an hour beforehand, yet still ran along the finishing chute to motivate me the last 300 yards.

After crossing the finish line, I collapsed onto a grass field. As I questioned my lack of strategy and lack of fitness while writhing in pain under a pop-up tent to get out of the heat, I knew I had a lot to learn before I brought up the idea of doing a full Ironman.

Dustin finished eighth overall.

Meanwhile, I finished next to last in my age group.

I hated how I felt right after that race. I knew I could do better. I would do better! Each race, I could improve and learn, especially about nutrition. And dang it, I wasn't going to get beat by someone with a bigger spare tire than mine ever again. And I certainly wasn't going to make another athlete fall off this bike and have a miserable race.

# Surprise! Let's Do an Ironman

About three months after Chattanooga, the pain and despair had worn off. I started dropping little hints to Dustin and our families about doing a full Ironman.

My wife's father Dave had recovered and was working out again. Although he still couldn't run very well, his knee was doing better. He was able to swim like a fish and bike like a jet, so my idea was becoming more plausible. Ever since watching him get so close in Ironman Lake Placid, I wanted a race somewhere close, with a flat course, and one our families could enjoy while we tried to kill ourselves over a seventeen-hour period.

Dustin was giddy with excitement. The second I said, "Hey, I've been thinking," he was in. We did our research, saved up some money, and planned to sign up for two races in 2020. Yup, I said two. Not only did we have the great idea of signing up for a full Ironman, but we decided it would be an inspiring idea to sign up for a half-Ironman at the same course a few months prior, as a dry run before the big dance.

I'll never forget calling Dave.

"Hey, Dave, I've been thinking . . . Dustin and I have been training pretty hard for about a year now. I think I want to do an Ironman."

After a long pause, he said, "Ahhhh, okay? Are you sure you want to do that?"

"Yes, absolutely certain. And we want you to join us!"

There was another pause.

"Dave, I know you were so close to finishing Lake Placid, and I'm gonna run this race for you, even if you can't make it. If your body can't handle it, I'll finish for you, but if you think you can make it, I want you in this race with me. I want to cross the finish line with you, hands raised together in glory, as you complete this lifelong dream of yours."

When I made the call, I knew one thing: Dave never backs down from a challenge. I also knew as time went on, his memory of the pain and disappointment would subside. I knew Dave never does anything half-assed. If I could just get him thinking about it, he would do everything possible to race with us.

In November, Dustin and I dropped the coin and locked into Ironman Gulf Coast 70.3 and Ironman Florida for the following year, 2020.

If you haven't signed up for an Ironman yet, let me tell you a few things. First, you have to sign up a full year in advance, especially for popular races like Ironman Florida. After registration opens, the athlete slots fill up in less than a month. Second, it is expensive! I felt like I was buying a new car, sight unseen. A half-Ironman is $350, and a full Ironman is $750. Then you have to buy race clothes, a really good bike that will last 112 miles, bike shoes, bike helmet, spare tires, running shoes, running socks, running clothes, a wetsuit, a swim skin, and swim goggles.

Oh, and don't forget a bike trainer. It's hard to find a road in Mississippi that doesn't have 100 trucks on forty-eight-inch tires doing eighty miles an hour on two-lane back roads where you ride. You have to set up in the garage and ride in one spot never actually going anywhere for three, four, or even five hours at a time.

Ironman is expensive and time consuming. All the while, you are spending tons of money for a race that could last up to seventeen hours, if you finish. That's if your bike doesn't break, if the sharks don't eat you, if you don't collapse on the run from pure exhaustion. So yeah, dropping all that money is pretty tough, but look on the bright side: you'll get maximum bang for your buck.

After spending all that money, a silver lining appeared. Dave was in! Well, he was in and out and then in again, but he agreed to sign up.

Another really important thing to consider before signing up for an Ironman is your family and support system. When I first told Kelli my plan, she was pissed that I was going to drag her dad back into a second Ironman. Moreover, she was pissed because growing up with her father competing, she knew the amount of time that I was going to need to train for the upcoming races.

After a few days of fuming, she calmed down and said, "I understand why you want to do this, and I support you. I know you'll basically have a second job with training, and I want you to know that I'll pick up the slack with the kids and be behind you every second of the way."

What an awesome wife! I couldn't have gone through all the training with a wife who loathed what I was doing every time I stepped out for a morning jog or who resented me every time I missed a dance practice because I had to ride the bike for four hours. Kelli is my rock. She not only puts up with my crap, but she is proud of me for what I do. I honestly could never have done any of this without her and my kids' support.

The night before we got married, Kelli came to me and said, "Alright, this is it. You've got me for life. We are never getting divorced. We will work all our problems out and talk through whatever we have to, but this is it. I don't want anybody else, and I hope you feel the same way. We are stuck with each other to the grave!"

Right then and there, I knew I had someone special. I knew our marriage would last forever. Here we are fourteen years later, all the better from one single conversation. Good times and bad, hard and easy . . . we've committed to always support and defend each other, to always be there for the other in times of need. We love life and everything that comes with it. Together we've discovered that as we love each other and are dedicated to each other, unimaginable feats become checked-off items on our bucket lists.

Ironman was a go, and Kelli was a go.

Life was good.

And it still is.

# I Love it When a Plan Comes Together

Dustin and I hammered out a training schedule. Ironman Gulf Coast 70.3 was slated for May 2020. Ironman Florida followed in November 2020. The experienced triathlete, Dave, told us to set up a six-day-a-week workout plan. This plan included one short, one medium, and one long session for each discipline. Three swims, three bikes, and three runs per week. Yes, nine workouts a week!

I'm not great at math, but I do know that nine workouts doesn't go into six days very well. I also know who my wife is. Let me tell you, this plan was not discussed with her first. Best to ask for forgiveness later in this instance.

To get the nine workouts in, we knew it'd take "bricks," a combination workout of two or more disciplines back-to-back. The goal was to get as close to ten hours of training per week. Most "experts" on the triathlon websites and message boards prescribe this.

When you put it down on paper, it looks like a daunting task.

But looks can be deceiving. It's impossible!

As an Air Force pilot, sometimes I fly at 4:30 a.m. and other times I fly at 7 p.m. My schedule changes day to day. Getting on a hard and fast schedule is intimidating and frustrating. Some days I'd wake up and work out at 5 a.m. before I flew. Other days I'd grab a quick run or bike between flights around lunch. Still, other days I'd find myself on the bike trainer at dinner time. Hell, some days I just said "screw it" and didn't do anything at all.

When you throw in vacations, sicknesses, birthday parties, and extra-long workdays, those ten planned hours of workouts for the week turn into one six-mile run every seven days.

Having an Excel spreadsheet of your workout plan printed next to your bathroom mirror keeps you honest. Well…it makes you feel guilty when you miss a workout. It's a necessary evil and in the long run it worked for me.

Training for an Ironman is not a game. It's a job. As I described above, a ten-hour-a-week workout is what most professionals prescribe. With a full-time job, the kid's activities, and responsibilities as a dad to help raise your kids right, it is imperative to plan your schedule early.

One thing to understand, there is no perfect way to train. People train differently, and it's okay. Some people do tons of intervals and mix in long workouts. Others simply go for distance and don't worry about speed. Still, others use heart-rate training.

Others go as hard as they can for as long as they can every single workout.

You have to find what's right for you. You need to know what is best for your body, and what it can handle. It might not be a bad idea to pay a professional or get a coach to build a training plan for you. It all depends on what you want to accomplish and how much you are willing to spend.

I thought I knew what was right for me, but hindsight is 20/20. All I wanted to do was finish. I knew I wasn't going to break any land speed records. I wish I would have mixed in more speed intervals with my long slow-distance workouts. I didn't have the perfect plan by any means, but this is how I decided to do it.

I created an Excel spreadsheet using landscape formatting. I set up rows for each week and columns for each day. The calendar started around eight months prior to the Ironman. My first day of each week started Monday. I filled out the competitions first, starting with Ironman Florida in the last row. From there, I worked backwards filling in gaps with smaller races, vacations, travel, and miscellaneous items already set in stone.

Dustin and I got together and picked several dates for long workouts. We also set aside weekends to go on training trips. I marked Sundays as my rest day. Life can be hectic. Sometimes the rest day came when my body told me it was time. Finally, I filled in the blanks on my spreadsheet for each week with a brick for short workouts and then one medium and one long run, bike, and swim.

Early on, the training was very difficult. In month one, we were only running three to five miles, swimming a thousand yards, and biking ten miles. Although these seem like miniscule distances compared to what's needed, we were preparing our bodies for the long haul.

If you haven't worked out six days straight in a while, you might've forgotten how bad the soreness can be after week one. Your legs ache, your body feels sluggish and stiff, and it's very hard to motivate yourself to get off the couch.

Several times during the first month, I gave myself a motivational speech to go run or swim in the early morning hours. I looked like the meme of the guy pointing at himself in the mirror and saying, "You're going to get off your lazy butt and get moving this morning!"

The best part about having a schedule staring you in the face every day is the amount of guilt you feel when you miss a workout. It is worse than the soreness you feel if you get it done.

Each morning once I put on my workout clothes, I was good. Workout clothes on, the workout was going to happen. At night, I would pack my bag and sit it right in front of the door leading to my garage. This mentally prepped me for the next day and wouldn't let me "forget."

When I hit the second month, I ramped things up. At this point, I had worked out four weeks in a row, almost every day. The initial soreness and shock to the body had worn off. I was seeing massive improvement with every swim, bike, and run. I was hitting my groove. At the end of the third month, I started to notice that I didn't feel right unless I completed a workout. After three months of training, your body starts to feel different. You are sore, but it's a good sore, not the debilitating kind you felt after week one.

Your muscles are tight, and you can feel the fibers stretch and retract. It's like they are super thick rubber bands stretched to the max and finely tuned. Longer distances became easier. The three-mile runs and twenty-five-mile bikes that used to destroy me now felt like easy warm-ups.

I started planning my days around workouts and craved the next time when I could enjoy some fresh air while breaking a sweat. It became addictive.

Also essential to my training were my partners: Dave and Dustin. Dave was my free online coach, and Dustin was my personal trainer. Always there, always ready. Without them, I never would have made it. Although five hours away, Dave was always available to answer questions in a quick phone call or text. He got daily snapshots of my Garmin workout summaries. Having someone to celebrate with and keep you accountable makes all the difference. It doesn't even have to be an athlete.

Training becomes something you love and loathe at the same time. It's not the workouts getting harder or running the same courses over and over. It's simply the time required to get in the distances you need. Like I said before, the training becomes a job. You have to do it, or you will never survive the race.

The training is the toughest part of the entire process. Your body feels amazing as you push into the later months. You crave the soreness and freedom of the road, trail, or water. It won't always be pretty. You won't always feel like an Olympian. But know that you are improving each day and making gains for the ultimate goal.

It's not all rainbows and cupcakes. You are going to have bad days. You are going to have bad weeks. Heck, you might even miss working out for two weeks because life gets in the way. Even worse, you might decide to quit in the middle of it because a worldwide pandemic keeps cancelling your races!

Dave told me at the very beginning, "If you need to take a break, take it." He was right, as always. Only you know your body and what it needs. Pay attention to it, work it to the max, but treat yourself with care.

If you need to slow things down or take several days off, it's okay! I found myself getting so wrapped up in the training and feeling so good, that I wanted to go hard and fast all the time. Every time I did that, my body would break down quicker. And in the end, that meant more down days.

Until Dustin and Dave introduced me to LSD.

Yup, I had the same reaction you just did. But when it comes to workouts, LSD stands for Long Slow

Distances. I thought Dustin had made it up because he needed drugs to run with me, since I was so much slower than him! But no, it's a legit way to train for an Ironman. LSDs keep your heart rate down and allow your body to get used to working out for long hours. It's the workout needed to ensure your body can keep moving for fifteen or more hours come race day.

When you sign up for an Ironman, what you're really signing up for is the training. It's crazy and feels like a job. You need partners to join you. You need to ensure you have different courses to choose from. Life is going to get in the way and you are going to have breaks, but again…that's okay as long as you get back in the saddle and don't lose sight of the end goal. Don't crush yourself every workout. Take it slow, and your body will reward you over the long haul. Most of all, enjoy it!

The one bond that holds all Ironmen together is the training. It's the one thing that makes us different. While other people may lift weights or run or bike, none of them do it all for five to six hours on Saturday mornings.

All triathletes share the unspoken respect that we work harder than anyone else. We go above and beyond normal daily routines and, yes, we are all a little bit crazy! We also start looking pretty good too! You can spot a triathlete from miles away. And, if you're lucky, your significant other will start to notice the transformation as well.

# My First Marathon

The first major hurdle in completing an Ironman was making sure I could complete a stand-alone marathon. Dustin and I chose the Louisiana Marathon in Baton Rouge slated for January 19, 2020.

Dustin had completed one marathon when he was younger. He told me it was the worst he had ever felt in a race. Halfway through, he said his legs cramped up and turned to stone. He was also running seven-minute miles, so I didn't feel bad for him. I would be taking my time, slowly getting through it. That's exactly what I did.

The day before the marathon, Dustin and I packed all our gear, then climbed into our respective family cars with the wives and kids. Once we were on the road, Dustin and I naturally raced each other for the entire five-hour drive.

For the first time ever, I won a race against Dustin! Mostly because I made my family "hold it" for longer than Dustin did. Either way, I got there first.

As I got keys for our rooms, Dustin asked if I had reserved the presidential suite for him. I laughed and said I was only a gold member at Hilton properties so there was no way I'd get *that* room. I told him, "Dream on, chump. This hotel doesn't even have a suite."

An elevator ride and a walk down the hall later, we pulled into our room. And there before us was a spacious corner room on the top floor with a picture on the wall of President Barak Obama, standing with staff members. We got the presidential suite! Ok, so the "picture" was just an eight by ten Walmart frame with a photo printed on standard white paper and no matting. But still, this looked like the presidential suite to us.

My wife and I laughed so hard we were rolling on the floor. I took a picture for Dustin and I rubbed it in his face. I not only won the race to Louisiana, but also got to spend the night with a picture of the president of the United States!

Traveling to races always comes with fun stories and experiences. This one would be no different. The night before the race, I learned a little something about myself.

We went to Olive Garden for dinner. Dustin and I had eaten at an Olive Garden before the Tuscaloosa half-marathon the year before. It worked out okay then, so we stuck with what we knew. I'm not a big guy. I'm 5'8" and about 175 pounds on a good week. I'm not extremely fit, but not fat. Everyone in my family except my mom is over six feet tall. I'm used to short jokes even though I'm not that short by today's standards. I say this because at age forty, the little guy jokes have mostly gone away…until we went to Olive Garden.

When the waitress brought out our water glasses, she gave me a kids-sized cup. She told us the dishes were being washed, and they didn't have enough big cups. Everyone at the table had a big cup except me, including my elementary-aged daughters.

Then, when the food came out, my pasta, which is usually served in a huge bowl, came out in a cereal bowl. At this point, I'm thinking something is up and the waitress is making fun of me for being a "little" guy. I get pissed, which is not normal for me. Dustin, his wife, my wife, and the kids are all laughing their asses off. So, I threw a napkin into my collar and ate like the five-year-old the server perceived me to be.

I don't know why, but it irked me to no end. It was the night before my first marathon, and I was getting served like a child. I was red-faced, pissy, and flat-out mad. All I wanted was the biggest glass of water they had, and a plate the size of Texas with pasta on it. Instead, I got a sippy cup and a bowl the size of Rhode Island.

The waitress flat out did not like me from the get-go. I'm not sure what I did to deserve it. Maybe I reminded her of an ex-boyfriend or something. Who knows.

Either way, it turned into a big joke the rest of the night and ever since.

That night I learned two things. First, for some reason I'm really good at being the butt of most jokes. Second, I learned that I needed to chill out prior to races. Even though I didn't think I was stressed or amped up about the race, I was! Apparently, our waitress picked up on that stress immediately. I try to keep a calm demeanor, but the smallest little thing can set me off. It's funny. I wasn't going to break any huge records or do something spectacular. I was going to run a four-hour marathon in preparation for an Ironman. Either way, everyone had a good laugh at my expense, and the meal turned out to be entertaining.

Race day came. The weather was perfect. It was forty degrees in the morning before the sun came up. Weather forecasters predicted it would be around fifty-five degrees about the time I expected to reach the finish line. I remembered to charge my watch and headphones correctly this time, using a wall plug and not a lamp. Lastly, I was hydrated.

Oh boy, was I hydrated.

The gun went off at the starting line and not thirty strides into the run, I had to pee! "You have got to be kidding me!" I thought I had learned my lesson from the Chattanooga triathlon. I didn't drink nearly enough before or during that race, but this was ridiculous. I hit the Porta Potty at mile one, then again at mile five, and again at mile ten. Luckily, as I listened to *Killer Angels* about the Battle of Gettysburg, I settled into a good pace and was feeling great. As author Michael Shaara gave first-person recollections from all the generals, I was able to ignore the call of nature.

At the halfway point, I made fun of all the "weak people" who were finishing the half-marathon portion and trudged on. Before I knew it, I was at mile twenty.

Mile twenty is when some weird, unexplained thing happens to us normal folk. First, my watch died…of course. I didn't realize the amount of power it took for the watch to play a book on tape using Bluetooth to connect to headphones. I should have expected this from my previous issues with technology.

Second, I got to see the race leaders pass me going the other direction. Holy crap! These guys were absolutely flying. It was a sight to see. They all looked so natural and smooth. And at the same time, they all looked like death, pushing their bodies to the absolute brink of exhaustion.

Third, I noticed I couldn't feel my legs anymore. I looked down and they were moving themselves. They didn't hurt, but it was weird to see my legs moving while my brain had nothing in it. I was involuntarily running at this point. Endurance races are great, but you have some weird sensations after the three-hour mark.

Inside of a mile to go, I spotted a guy in front of me who I realized had been with me almost the entire race. We would pass each other every now and again. After the last aid station, he had been in front of me for about three miles. I remember he had on a white hat turned backwards and a white T-shirt.

I decided I was going to beat him to the finish line.

I pulled up next to him on the final straight away.

He looked at me and said, "Hell, no!"

He then proceeded to take off as fast as lightning. I chased him down best as I could, but he beat me by about three steps.

After we crossed the finish line, both of us had a great laugh. Even though we never spoke during the race, he said he knew I was there the entire time. We gave each other a high five and a congratulatory back slap.

Dustin finished the race in three hours and thirty minutes. I finished the race in four hours and ten minutes. But Dustin looked like death after the race. I had been waiting for "the machine" to show some chinks in his armor, and he finally did. He couldn't stop shivering and literally passed out on the drive home. I finished and had a beer!

What a great lead-in for Ironman. Now I knew I could run a marathon. All I had to do was swim 2.4 miles and bike 112 miles beforehand.

No sweat!

One of the great things about the Louisiana Marathon was the people. All along the neighborhood streets, people would set out tables of ice, water, and Gatorade. People had their dogs out on the street. They had funny signs about peeing while you run and, at mile thirteen, "You're only halfway there" signs. It was a great atmosphere and a fun race. About four miles from the finish line, one family had the greatest table I've ever seen. It had a giant glass bowl of Motrin followed by fifty shots of whiskey, fifty more shots of vodka, and another giant glass bowl, this time full of Tylenol. What a perfect table for the end of a marathon.

I held a shot of whiskey in hand for about two seconds, then thought better of it.

Looking back on it, maybe that shot would have shaved ten minutes off my time for an even four-hour finish. I guess we'll never know, but there's always next time! I thought to myself as I watched Dustin walk around like a zombie, shivering under a tin foil blanket, if maybe the shot of whiskey might've helped him…or maybe it was his downfall. I found out later he had pushed himself to the brink. Remember, he only has one speed.

# **Grinding to a Halt**

February rolled in hot with some weird occurrences and craziness. My wife got sick as a dog for a week after we returned from vacation. I locked her in our room upstairs and wouldn't let the kids go anywhere near her for fear of the whole house getting sick. This was before all the COVID-19 cases started popping up like crazy in March. Looking back on it, she had all the symptoms. She had trouble breathing. She had a fever and no taste or appetite. After a week of sickness and a trip to the emergency room, she finally got through it. By an act of God, the girls and I didn't catch whatever she had. My training, on the other hand, took an unscheduled vacation.

When Kelli fully recovered a few weeks later, Dustin and I hit the training plan hard. The Ironman Gulf Coast 70.3 was only eight weeks out. We had set a one-year training regimen for the full Ironman in

November. We were almost five solid months into the process. We tried our hardest to schedule ahead for long runs and bikes on weekends. Those grand plans soon grinded to a halt.

As we all know, COVID-19 came with a vengeance.

Dustin went down hard with the virus. This was before vaccines. Life was rough back then. You never knew how the body was going to react and we were all witnessing the effects firsthand as the virus spread. Dustin was sitting around the pool with several families one afternoon, soaking up the sun and enjoying the warm weather. He woke up the next morning and felt like someone had hit him in the face with a brick tied to the end of a rope. I did not see him or talk to him for the next five days. We were all in isolation because of exposure. When he finally emerged from his house to get the mail after five days,

I thought the zombie apocalypse was upon us. He looked like Ichabod Crain cast as the lead in a zombie movie, slowly lurching out to his mailbox. Needless to say, I kept my distance a little while longer.

Our work schedules became super inconsistent and erratic. We couldn't be around anyone or go anywhere.

On top of that, we started getting emails about races cancelling, asking if we wanted to defer to next year's edition.

Now, I don't know about you, but I need a definitive race on the calendar. Otherwise, you can flat-out forget about me training.

I lost all focus, I lost all motivation, and I went back to my three large pepperoni pizzas per week training plan. I was miserable not knowing if any of the races would go as scheduled.

We had to make a decision.

Either we would keep training because it was the right thing and hope the races might happen. Or we could trash it all and venture back into lazy, fat mode.

Dustin and I chose the latter . . . let me rephrase, I chose the latter for about a full month.

I did absolutely nothing the entire month of March. I ran four total three-mile runs.

Here's the funny thing about training for an Ironman. It changes you! You find yourself itching for the next run or bike. You get depressed when you don't workout. Laziness makes body parts start hurting again. You get stiff and your body craves that soreness from continuous motion.

I can tell you—as possibly the laziest person on the planet—March 2020 was one of the worst months I've had in a long time. I felt depressed, drank a ton of

White Claws and Bud Light, ate too much, and stayed irritable most of the time.

All the training I had been doing all the way back to early 2019 fell apart.

I lost every single gain I made. When I finally got back on the horse, it was like starting from ground zero.

# Motivation from the One and Only

March came and went. In April something good finally happened. Dustin retired from the Air Force after twenty years of service to our great nation. I decided to do something special for him. I wrote to every single United States president he had served under, from Bill Clinton to Donald Trump, and got letters of appreciation personally signed by each one.

That wasn't the coolest part though.

I had been listening to Mike Reilly's new book *Finding My Voice*. If you don't know who Mike Reilly is, I highly suggest you grab his book. Or listen to it on audiobook, which he narrates himself. Mike Reilly is the crazy guy at the finish line of every Ironman you've seen on television. You will find him waving towels, playing loud music, and pumping up the crowd. The guy shows up at every race at 4 a.m. and wouldn't dare leave before the seventeen-hour cut off time. The cut off usually happens at the stroke of midnight. He helps motivate athletes across the finish line. He tells the crowd stories about special athletes finishing. And he does what he is most famous for: Yelling in his unmistakable scratchy voice as each participant crosses the finish line, "YOU ARE AN IRONMAN!"

That is, if you are lucky enough to finish a full Ironman.

Anyway, I searched his website and sent a message asking if there was anything he could do as a gift for my best friend. Mike wrote me back immediately and asked if a signed copy of his book would be a good gift for Dustin. I was floored. He took time out of his day to respond and shipped a signed copy of his book from California on express delivery!

To boot, Mike even called Dustin on his retirement date to say congratulations and thanked him for his service.

Mike Reilly is a class act. He pours his heart and soul into this crazy sport we all love. He treats everyone with respect. He makes everyone feel as though you are his best friend. On the course and off, people like Mike, make triathlon the sport it has become. Very rarely in this sport will you find a turd. Everyone is rooting for each other. Professionals will stop and talk to you after the race, and the volunteers are second to none. I thanked Mike for his generosity and for motivating me again through his actions and his book.

His last message to me was, "I can't wait to see you and Dustin at the finish line and tell you both that you are IRONMEN!"

# Back on the Horse

Motivated and no longer under lockdown, Dustin and I started training again in April. I was ready to start feeling better. The Ironman Gulf Coast 70.3 cancelled. We deferred our registration to a race in Augusta, Georgia, but it cancelled as well. Finally, we moved our registration to Ironman Chattanooga 70.3 in May 2021. Looking back on it, that was the smartest thing we could have ever done.

If you remember in my opening, I said that there are no regrets. I also believe there are no coincidences. You can call me crazy and I'm okay with that. Corny, I know, but have you ever seen the movie *Signs* with Mel Gibson? Two main characters are sitting on the couch having a conversation about coincidences. People either think they are real or they believe everything has a purpose and meaning. I'm on the purpose and meaning side of thinking. In my forty years of life, I've seen too many extraordinary things happen to believe it was all luck and chance.

Whether you believe in a higher power or not, I truly believe that we are destined to become certain people and do certain things when the time is right. There are no coincidences. For example, if my lazy ass would have done a half Ironman six months before a full in 2019, I would have asked for a refund when all the 2020 cancellations started rolling out! I definitely wouldn't be writing this book right now.

Dave warned me about doing a half Ironman first. He said, "Remember, if you are going to do it, treat it like a training session for the full. Don't get discouraged on mile fifty-six of the bike thinking, "Oh no, I have to do that distance all over again and then run a marathon in six months!" He was right!

Which leads me to my next point. Listen to your elders! They know what they're talking about.

During the following weeks, Dustin and I would run in the mornings and go to the local YMCA pool in the afternoons. We ran in the mornings because it was so hot after 8 a.m. that you would start sweating before putting on your shoes. If we missed the morning, we would wait until dusk.

I don't know if you've ever experienced Mississippi in late spring and summer, but holy crap! I've been to the Middle East several times for work, I've been to the desert in the southwest United States, and I've been on vacation to Mexico and the Bahamas. Not a single one of these places holds a straw to the heat in Columbus, Mississippi. It's like someone took a towel out of scalding hot water and draped it over everyone and everything. It takes you twenty minutes of standing naked under a fan after you shower to stop sweating.

My favorite workouts were early morning swims at the base pool. I would do this workout when I didn't feel like running. There's something about getting to the pool at 5 a.m. The sky is beautiful blue that fades to black as you look toward the western horizon. The pool looks like glass, and the lights put a calming ambiance in the water. I said earlier that I hated morning workouts. I still hate waking up early, but I relish these early morning outdoor pool swims. It is such a great way to start the day. These workouts made the swim my favorite discipline, even though I'm slow as molasses.

On runs, Dustin and I would go together as much as possible. We utilized the neighborhood on the Air Force base for simplicity. We had tracks set up for any distance. We knew that if you ran to the first stop sign and back, it would be exactly two miles. If you passed the stop sign, went into three cul-de-sacs, and then passed Ms. Patty's horse farm, you could get six miles. If you ran around the airfield on base, it was twelve miles. And if you ventured out into Tupelo and ran the Tanglefoot Trail, you'd have to turn around. Everyone thinks it's a great idea to chain their 250-pound pit bulls to chains next to that trail. It's Mississippi, what can I say.

My most memorable training experiences were running the trails at Lake Lurlene State Park in Tuscaloosa, Alabama. I also really enjoyed biking the Natchez Trace highway from Tupelo, Mississippi, to the Alabama state line and back. After running and biking the same roads day in and day out, finding destination training sites became something Dustin and I coveted.

We went to Lake Lurlene in Alabama and ran a four-mile loop twice. It was beautiful. It reminded me of Kennesaw Mountain in Georgia with Dave. It was quiet, wooded, and peaceful. No headphones, just a soft trail with rolling hills and my best friend. The trick was to always make Dustin run in front. As much as I love that dude, I'd rather him get bit by the snake than me! At least four miles of the run consisted of conversations about what we would do when we ran into a snake. Luckily, it never happened, although I'm sure eventually it will.

The bike ride on the Natchez Trace was great. We started in the heart of Tupelo and rode northeast to the Alabama state line. At this point, both of us needed to get in a century ride, one hundred miles. The foothills of the Appalachians provided us the distance. We were both sick of the 17.6-mile course on the Air Force base and sure as hell weren't going to ride the roads in our hometown.

You might as well go run the hallways of your local prison during break time. Actually, that might be safer than the roads of Mississippi with stray dogs and monster trucks. Not to mention the potholes that look like portals to China.

So, off we went on our first one hundred miler! We both had four bottles of water and Liquid IV. I had protein bars and peanut butter and jelly sandwiches shoved into the back of my bike jersey. The bikes were cleaned, tuned, and ready to rock.

I almost forgot. After the Chattanooga triathlon, Dustin helped me find a triathlon bike. I got a used one for $600 on Facebook Marketplace. It was a 2016 Orbea Ordu with basic components. You want a tri bike if you plan to do an Ironman. Once you get comfortable in the aero position, it's the only way to ride for long distances. The tri bike moves your hips forward compared to a normal road bike. It places your body over the pedals instead of behind them. This allows you to have more power and less fatigue over the course of the race. It engages your muscles differently so you can immediately run afterwards without your legs feeling like wet noodles.

Speaking of comfortable, I've never been comfortable on a bike.

You remember my story of making the guy fall off of his bike during the Chattanooga race? Well, I had my own little crash not long after.

I was riding in the neighborhood, when one of my neighbors pulled up to a stop sign at the top of our street. I was decked out in spandex, trying to look cool and nonchalant. I stuck my hand out to let them know I would be turning left onto the street where they were stopped. As I hit the intersection, I encountered a massive pile of gravel and BOOM, "Down Goes Frazier!" I was too dumb to unclip from my pedals, so I skid across the rough blacktop. It sure would be nice if clip-in-pedals came with in-person egress training! That would have saved me some pain over the years.

I immediately hop up, trying hard not to look like an idiot. I see the friend in her minivan with a "What in the hell just happened?" look on her face.

She rolls the window down and asks if I'm okay. I wave her off. She drives off and then the guy who lives on the corner appears like an apparition. At this point I'm so embarrassed, I don't know what to do, so I check myself over and make sure nothing's broken. The guy who lives on the corner asks if I need anything.

As the pain set in, I said "maybe a little bit of pride."

He laughed and walked off. I got home and stripped off my torn spandex.

It was nasty. I had road rash from my calf all the way up my left side to the top of my shoulder.

My wife said I looked like a cougar had mauled me.

I told her she hadn't been with me all day!

As a nurse, she took care of me. She scrubbed all the gravel out, iced me down, and loaded me up with Tylenol. I didn't realize it until later, but the end of my handlebar had gone directly into my groin region. The pain wouldn't present itself until that night, when the adrenaline wore off. And oh, I had a half-marathon scheduled seven days later.

If you haven't figured it out, I hate biking. This is just one of the reasons why.

I finished that half-marathon in Birmingham seven days later, with a pulled or damaged groin. I never got it checked out. I told you I was stubborn and

I never quit. I never give up on anything. It's probably one of my biggest faults and blessings at the same time.

Fast forward back to the century ride with Dustin. Twenty-four miles in, we found a rest area and pulled over to eat a snack and grab some water. As I pull over to the side of the curb, my dumbass forgets to unclip my right shoe once again. After coming to a stop, I toppled over into the grass with my bike landing on top of me.

"You have got to be shitting me!"

And what did Dustin do? He helped me up, dusted me off, and made sure I was okay, right?

Nope, he pulled out his phone and took a picture of me lying flat on my back. My bike was on top of me, and I obviously had a pissed off look on my face.

What an ass!

For the last fifteen miles before the turn around, we encountered hills.

Try to picture this.

Me, the guy who can barely handle a bike, doing forty miles per hour down a giant hill. I looked like a leaf in the wind, wobbling and shaking. I have not been that scared in my entire life. You better believe I wasn't going to hit the brakes though! With every downhill usually comes an uphill, and momentum is key.

The hills and the ride slowly continued and I gained confidence with every mile. We somehow, by the grace of God, made it back to Dustin's truck one hundred miles later. I was still in one piece. Along the way, we took a bunch of fun pictures to include one at the Alabama state line sign. I sent that picture to Mike

Reilly to show him I was ready for Ironman Florida. He texted me back and said he would be waiting.

At this point, I had run a marathon and biked one hundred miles.

Now I had to figure out if I could do them back-to-back.

# Running Short on Time

Training hit full tilt. We weren't getting the prescribed ten hours a week, but we were doing our best. My Excel spreadsheet was filling up with accomplished distances and times. I had completed what felt like thousands of workouts: anywhere from 3 to 20 miles on runs, 500 to 4,200 yards on swims, and 16 to 100 miles on the bike. Only six weeks remained, and I was feeling good!

Then an unexpected phone call came.

Dave had been running with his friends at Kennesaw Mountain like he had hundreds of times before. But this time he collapsed. The details were fuzzy at first due to the chaos of the situation. Dave stopped for a drink of water. After the first gulp, he fell flat on his face . . . out like a light. Another runner on the trail, who happened to be a nurse, came along within minutes. They performed CPR on him because they couldn't feel a pulse. After several attempts and a few heart-wrenching minutes later, the group finally found a weak pulse. Dave started moving in and out of consciousness. They called for an ambulance. Luckily, they were close to one of the roads that wind through the park. Eventually, an ambulance arrived, and EMTs were able to reach him with a gurney to get him in the ambulance and to the hospital.

Do you remember what I said about coincidences?

Let me say that again. A nurse happened to be walking by Dave in the early morning hours at Kennesaw Mountain. This happened the exact time he collapsed…that didn't happen by chance. He also collapsed within a quarter mile of a main road. He very well could have dropped halfway up the mountain where a recovery would have been near impossible. That didn't happen by chance either!

They transported Dave to the hospital and he stayed for several days. I don't know how he survived it, but he had us all scared stiff. With the little bit of information gathered at the beginning, everyone was panicking. Especially the first several hours. Long story short, he had a drop in blood pressure that knocked him out cold. Another unknown issue caused his pulse to be too weak to find, but no one knew that at the time. Dave, the person who got me into this whole triathlon thing, was OUT!

No more racing for Dave, this was the final straw.

# The Miraculous Comeback

Well…it wasn't quite the final straw. Dave put the same amount of effort into meeting with doctors and recovering as he did training. Come to find out, there was no heart defect or crazy disease. It was something he could control with diet.

You see, Dave, like me, is a sweater.

I don't mean the warm things you wear in the winter. And I don't mean a little wet under the arms either. When Dave and I run, we look like we climbed out of a pool after three measly miles. Everyone's physiology is different. When the heat and humidity get unbearable in the summer, Dave sweats. When you sweat like Dave and I do, creating a misting station for anyone within five feet of you, you also lose salt. When you lose salt, your blood thins out. When your blood thins out, your heart must pump harder and when your heart pumps too hard, you pass out! Simple enough.

So, like I said, Dave was out. But after several doctor's visits and testing, new salt tablets and electrolyte drink mixes, he was back in. Dave's wife wasn't too happy, and his daughter, my wife, wasn't too happy either. They both knew it was going to take a lot more than passing out, losing blood pressure, riding in an ambulance, and taking a five-day, insurance-paid training break to keep him from Ironman Florida. Nevertheless, neither one were going to celebrate his decision.

Did I mention Dave is a little crazy? Like most of us, he can drive others crazy as well.

Dave started his training circuit again, slowly, and made a pact with the family and me. He said he would walk the marathon portion of the Ironman.

Under normal circumstances, this isn't a great strategy. In Dave's case, it was a great one. He is a natural swimmer and his bike speeds are off the charts. He knew that if he had a good swim and a great bike, he would finish the marathon in plenty of time to finally become an Ironman. Even if he walked the entire thing. His race day strategy was set, his promise to loved ones was etched in stone, and in record time he was back to training.

# Florida Bound

Dustin, Dave, and I booked a giant four-bedroom condo in Panama City Beach, Florida, for Thursday through Tuesday with the race being on Saturday, November 7. Dustin and I drove down together and met up with Dave and Barbara Thursday night. Dustin's family and my wife and kids came down the next day so they wouldn't miss school.

Again, the support team was in full effect. Kelli sent us down with her signature chicken noodle casserole, pre-cooked and frozen for the night before the race. Barbara did the same thing with her signature brown rice and chicken casserole for Thursday night. You've gotta love southern women and their healthy casseroles!

The drive down was great. Dustin and I were alone in his truck. We listened to loud music, told fun jokes, listened to *Iron War* on audiobook, and glanced in the rearview mirror at least 700 times to ensure our bikes were still secured to the rack. Before we knew it, the sweet smell of salt water and palm trees filled the air.

Upon arrival, we settled into the condo with Dave and Barbara, then walked down for check-in at the race expo. Due to all the COVID-19 protocols, we had to sign up for a check-in time weeks prior.

If you've ever seen the Ironman Village before big races, you know it's typical for swarms of the most fit people in the world to be buzzing around with $10,000 bikes as music blasts. It is a giant block party.

This year was weird. Everyone was socially distanced, wearing masks, and lining up to go through several check points to take temperatures and answer health screening questionnaires. Instead of masses of people congregating at one time, people trickled in according to their pre-assigned check-in times. Needless to say, I would have worn a bubble boy suit if that's what it was going to take for this race to go.

This race almost didn't go by the way. COVID-19 restrictions on large groups of people was a major hurdle. They also had to deal with federal and state regulations on testing and mask wear. If you remember, it was during this time when sports were slowly coming back, but no fans were allowed to attend. This was another point of contention, because Ironman draws a lot of spectators. The state of Florida, Ironman staff, and the city council had all been working together tirelessly to resolve these issues. About one month prior to the race, they said "To hell with it, we will do the best we can, put in protective measures, and hope people act responsibly." That's exactly what they did and that's exactly what happened.

Ironman Florida was the first race run in the United States since October 2019. A full year since the Kona Ironman World Championships. Hats off to the Ironman staff, the participating athletes, and the amazing volunteers who put the event on.

After check-in, we walked through the Ironman Village and visited the shop. This was one of the worst things for me to do. I was like a kid in a candy store looking at all the shirts, hats and workout gear. But there was no way in hell I was going to jinx myself by buying Ironman gear prior to finishing the race.

I'm not extremely superstitious, but that's one gamble I was not willing to take. I even skipped out on signing up for a really nice plaque you can get at the races. It has your medal, pictures of the course, a replica race bib, and your times all set up in a huge frame. If you order it before the race, you save twenty-five dollars.

NO WAY!

Dave and Dustin had a little more confidence than me and pre-ordered. I said I'd figure it out after I finished.

Check-in complete and having walked through the village, we headed back to the condo and started to get ready for Friday's light workouts before the race.

# The Last Training Session

Before our families arrived on Friday morning Dave, Dustin, and I got up around 5:30 a.m. and headed to the beach where the swim would start on race day. We jumped in the water and took a leisurely swim to the end of the pier, which was only a quarter of what we would have to swim the next day. It was really nice to test out the water and the waves and ensure my wetsuit was perfectly fit.

Speaking of wetsuits, I almost forgot to tell you about my wetsuit test swim back in Mississippi. Wetsuits are pretty awesome. They make you super buoyant and fast. You generally can subtract five seconds off of your 100-yard pace by wearing one. I had never swum in a wetsuit before, and no outdoor pools were open in October. I joined the local YMCA after the military base pool shutdown for the summer. It was a great place to swim with multiple chances for laps during the week. It was an indoor pool and heated, so you could swim there year-round.

When I finally found the time to test out my wetsuit, I forgot that the water was anywhere from eighty-four to eighty-six degrees Fahrenheit. I jumped in and swam 4,000 yards.

About halfway through the swim, I realized I was feeling like absolute crap. I thought I hadn't had enough food or water. Maybe I was having an off day. When I finally pulled myself over the side of the pool like a beached whale, I stripped off the wetsuit as quickly as I could. I was sweating profusely and my whole body looked like a giant strawberry. I took a super cold shower and stepped on the scale.

In a two-hour swim, I had lost six pounds of water weight!

That's the crazy thing about swimming. Most newcomers don't think about it, but you sweat when you swim just like you do on the bike and run. A wetsuit in eighty-six-degree water is not smart. Please learn from my mistake and don't do it!

During the warm-up swim, the seventy-two-degree Gulf of Mexico waters near Panama City in early November were absolutely perfect. Our test swim was over and we all felt great.

As we exited the water and started walking up the beach towards the car, we noticed a crowd near the water. As we strolled over for a closer look, we saw a young man with Down Syndrome surrounded by coaches and family members. He was doing light swims in the ocean and being filmed by Ironman NOW television cameras. He was so happy, giving everyone hugs and waving. He looked like he was having the time of his life. It wasn't until after the race that we realized it was Chris Nikic, the first person with Down Syndrome to ever complete an Ironman.

If you haven't read his story or seen the news articles, go check it out. He was a headliner on the ESPN Espy Awards.

What an amazing feat of human performance for someone who the majority of the world thought didn't stand a chance. Even though Chris had competed in the Special Olympics and was obviously an amazing athlete, he had to overcome obstacles that Dustin and I will never fully experience or comprehend. He had an amazing team surrounding him and he did it. He took every stroke, pedal, and step. Hats off to Chris, his team, and his family. Although we weren't directly involved, it was amazing to witness a small portion of the work he put in to complete the race. We walked away motivated by Chris.

Next up was a nice little jaunt on the bike.

A nice little jaunt can have multiple meanings . . . as I soon came to find out. From my previous stories, you already know I hate biking. What I haven't told you in detail is how much Dustin and Dave L.O.V.E biking. We wanted to get a short ride in to make sure our gears were rotating smoothly and nothing was glaringly wrong with our equipment.

To Dave, this meant about twenty miles. To me, it meant three. We hit Thomas Drive along the coast and rode down to the end of the pier. Dave was out front by ten bike lengths at first, with Dustin shortly behind him, and then me acting as the anchor on this short voyage. We passed the condo, then came to a wonderful intersection that would have been a perfect turn-around spot. But Dave hit a new gear.

He exploded like a shot from a cannon. He was feeling good and wanted to ride. I, on the other hand, knew that I had to ride 112 miles the next day and wanted to save every ounce of misery for the race. I slowed way down and let Dave get away. Dustin kept looking back at me and I just shrugged my shoulders. Dave wasn't looking back. In fact, he had turned into a spec on the horizon.

I finally flagged down Dustin and said, "What the hell is he doing?" Dustin laughed and said he would go grab him. I turned around and went back to the hotel.

Both those turds beat me back to hotel because they had about six miles per hour on me, but I didn't mind. All I had to do was survive the bike and not crash on Saturday, then I could throw this darn thing into the dumpster!

We razzed Dave a little when we got back to the condo, and he took it pretty well. Because his knee was still pretty much shot and he planned on walking the marathon, he decided not to join us on the short two-mile run. Dustin and I jogged at a nine-minute, thirty-second-pace along the beach and soaked in the wonderful Florida sun.

I absolutely love the beach and it was a perfect setting to complete our training. Our last training session complete, we headed back to the condo and prepped for our families to arrive.

# Family Pizza Night a Day before the Ironman?

We showered and laid out our gear. Dustin decided to grab some food for the kids to have when they arrived. A pizza place was right across the street and we all know kids love pizza.

The problem is, so do I!

When I order a pizza, it always has extra cheese and pepperoni. Yes, this was my super healthy food choice right before the hardest race of my life! I ordered one large for the kids and one large for myself. As Dave looked sideways at me, I proceeded to down a twenty-ounce Diet Dr. Pepper, because why not! I had been drowning myself in water for months. I needed some flavor! I was in great shape and pizza has a lot of carbs and salt in it. I eat it all the time. How bad could it be?

In less than 24 hours, I would know the answer to that question.

I told you at the beginning: I am not a purist. I have my vices and I do a lot of stupid things. Food and soft drinks are a major vice. Oh yeah, I almost forgot about five chocolate chip cookies. The wife sent those . . . they were supposed to be for the kids. Uh oh!

The families arrived and we helped everyone unload the cars. Everyone settled into their rooms around 4 p.m. and we took the kids down to the beach. It was relaxing and fun. Everyone was in a great mood and the weather was perfect. The water was a little cold, but it didn't bother the kids at all. They surfed the tiny waves on their boogey boards while the rest of us relaxed in lawn chairs. Less than twelve hours till race time. It was about to get serious.

Depending on what kind of person you are and your desires for the race outcome, the nerves you feel the day before a race can be a little concerning.

For instance, Dave knew this was his last chance. He might have looked cool on the outside, but I knew he was a ball of nerves on the inside, understandably so. I, on the other hand, wasn't so much nervous as I was anxious to finally get the race started. After all the training and preparing my body, I felt ready. I just wanted to go.

Dustin, on the other hand, was somewhere in between. I couldn't really read his emotions because of that California cool attitude he usually wears. No matter where you fall on the spectrum, just know that eventually, the cannon is going to go off and you are going to start the race. Your body will be in the best shape it's ever been in. You will be ready, regardless of what your brain tells you.

In order to break up the nerves, I got an idea. We were on the beach, in a huge condo with glass windows all around. I turned on Bob Marley and the Whaler's greatest hits and opened all the sliding glass doors. The cool breeze, reggae music, and sound of the ocean in the distance floated through the condo. As soon as *Three Little Birds* blasted through the condo's speakers, the mood lightened. Suddenly everyone was in vacation mode.

It also didn't hurt that we had kids running around with huge smiles on their faces because they were at the beach.

# Packing the Gear

When you check in for the race, they give you several plastic bags for your gear. You get a white bag for morning clothes, a blue bag for the bike transition, and a red bag for the run transition. You also get two white bags, each for halfway on the bike and the run. Packing these bags isn't as easy as you'd think. You need to pack everything you'll need for 140.6 miles. These bags must carry all the necessities to ensure a successful race. Leaving one small thing out could be disastrous.

Weeks before the race, Dustin and I called each other twenty million times and made ten thousand in-house visits. We became obsessed ensuring we had everything needed. It got so bad, the wives started making fun of us.

Kelli would say, "What are you wearing tonight?" when she heard Dustin was coming to the house.

We made piles of clothes, nutrition, and equipment for each bag and spread them all over the bedroom floor. The biggest one was for bike transition. Shoes, helmet, glasses, water bottles, and nutrition takes up a lot of space. The run transition bag was less. It included socks, running shorts, a cotton T-shirt, race belt, and shoes. In the halfway bags, we put things we didn't mind getting thrown away. My bike halfway bag included extra tire tubes, water bottles, baby wipes, and a hand towel. The run halfway bag had Advil, hand towels, fresh socks, and a shirt.

I'm still steaming about the decision to use my favorite NASA shirt to start the run. It was the most comfortable shirt I've ever owned and a staple for every race. It was my "woobie." In case you don't have kids, a "woobie" is a blanket small children carry with them everywhere. I figured if it could make it through an Ironman, it would be a good time to retire old faithful. I thought I'd be able to get it back after the race, but I was too late. They told us not to expect getting some items back. I wish I would have chosen a different one, but I guess it died a good death! Unfortunately, all I have now is memories of "the one that got away."

We quadruple checked everything in our organized piles of clothes and equipment. Once our obsessive, compulsive sides were satisfied, everything went into a special suitcase. The night before the race, the equipment and clothing came back out and into piles again. We inventoried one final time and then put the gear into the correct colored bags. One great idea Dave gave us was to use colored duct tape to "decorate" our bags. I used lime green and an

American flag. It made finding our halfway bags much easier. Having something that sticks out in the midst of thousands of white bags at a race can save time and stress.

After we packed the bags one final time, another "incident" happened. I was doing a bike check. I placed my stickers in the right places and checked that my tires were inflated to one hundred pounds per square inch.

As I unscrewed the back plastic cap on my front tire valve, I heard a hiiiiiiisssssssss.

"You have got to be kidding me. What the heck!"

Dustin and Dave heard the racket and walked into my room to find me and my flat-tired bike sitting against the wall. After further inspection, we realized that the valve had unscrewed when I took it off the plastic cap. The only thing left was a metal extender that went into the tire. They ridiculed me for a solid thirty minutes.

Talk about losing your cool! I was hours away from racing and thought I had completely destroyed my bike with no one to fix it. I freaked out and started pacing the room. Luckily for me, Dustin is basically a bike mechanic. He retrieved the valve from inside the plastic cap. He screwed it back into the valve stem and pumped my tire back up in five minutes. Crisis averted, for now.

I knew this bike was going to try to kill me, mentally or physically, within the next twenty hours. It was already starting to taunt me. Satisfied with nothing broken, we went back to the transition area and dropped off our bikes.

I couldn't believe it. We were finally doing this.

Later that night we tried to go to bed early. We ended up watching the movie *McFarland* with our families. If you ever need a feel-good movie to inspire you, go check it out. Motivated, fed with chicken and rice casserole, and an hour of putting together my gear, I put on an audio book and hit the sack.

Most people can't sleep before big races. It makes sense. You are excited, giddy, and your body is tense with anxiety. You feel like you don't need sleep. You know you have to wake up around 4 a.m. You usually wake up every hour and look at your clock to see if it's time to go. For some unknown reason, it didn't happen to me that night. Maybe I was mentally exhausted from packing and thinking my bike had broken. I don't know. I went to sleep around 9:30 p.m. and woke up at 4 a.m. ready to roll.

# Ironman Florida Race Morning

When you wake up on Ironman morning, you don't slog out of bed. You leap out of bed. It reminded me of my kids on Christmas morning. They blast out of bed like two fog horns, screaming and running around like the world is on fire. Instead of "Santa Came, Santa Came!" we were whispering "Race Day, Race Day!" We didn't want to wake up the entire house. Dave, Dustin, and I all walked into the kitchen together. None of us said a word to each other for about thirty minutes. We each drank a cup of coffee, ate some oatmeal and a bagel, and choked down as much water as we could. I took a quick shower, lathered up in sunscreen, and out the door we went.

Going back to our support team for a minute. Barbara drove us down to the transition area at 4:45 a.m. I know this doesn't sound cosmic. The start line was two miles away. Even so, I was so impressed with the love and commitment everyone was giving us. Not only did our families suffer through a full year of training and traveling to races, they stood right next to us the whole way and gave us everything we could have ever wanted. They made life easy during our journey to greatness. Well, at least that's what we thought. I actually think our wives were more nervous than we were before the race. My wife didn't sleep a wink that night.

The transition area was a sight to see. The morning air was crisp. The sun was still hours from cresting the horizon. People were bustling around the racks of bikes. Swarms of the most highly-tuned athletes I'd ever seen were gathered in one place. People were walking around in wetsuits with the tops hanging below their waists. Others were pumping up their bike tires. Even more were chatting with their friends and doing one last check on all their gear and nutrition.

I went through my mental checklist and ensured everything was good to go. My bike tires were one hundred pounds per square inch. I had four water bottles, two of which had an electrolyte mix. My bike jersey, helmet, glasses, and shoes were laid out in perfect order for transition one. My running shoes, shorts, T-shirt, and queen-size bed sheet were on the other side of my bike for transition two.

Yes, I said a queen-size bed sheet. One COVID-19 protocol that changed how we raced was no more changing tents. In previous races, they had enclosed areas where you could change out of bike clothes and into run clothes. Protocols wouldn't allow that many people in an enclosed area. No public nudity allowed either. It was not uncommon to see a lot of bare rear ends at races in the past. This year, it was strictly prohibited and enforced. I read on Facebook where someone had a great idea. Throw a queen-sized sheet over your head and voila, a changing tent!

Most people wore a tri-suit under their wetsuit and didn't change for the race. I was bound and determined to get out of those spandex bike shorts and into some comfortable running shorts after 112 miles on the bike—not to mention, put on extra socks and a new T-shirt from the halfway bag of the marathon. I knew the only way I could make myself comfortable over a seventeen-hour workout was to race like I trained.

I also knew I wasn't going to set any world records, so comfort was king.

As the sun crested the horizon, a magical voice came over the loud speaker. Mr. Reilly was calling athletes to the swim start. Dustin, Dave, and I decided to go together with the two- minute per one-hundred-yard pace group. We walked in a long, snaking line that led from the parking lot. It crossed Thomas Drive and ended at the starting chutes on the beach. The walk took about thirty minutes in total. As we were waiting in line around 6:45 a.m., the mini-cannon exploded.

BOOM!

The pros hit the water and the crowd of more than 2,000 triathletes roared with excitement. We were finally back to Ironman racing!

# Jaws, Jellyfish, and Big Red Buoys

The white sugar-sand beaches were cold to the touch, the bright sun was rising in the east, and the view of the calm ocean lapping against the shore was serene. At the same time, loud music and Mike Reilly blared out of the speakers while athletes wearing fluorescent swim caps were bobbing up and down as far as the eye could see. It's the yin and yang of triathlon start lines. I like to call it calm chaos.

As we inched closer to the start, you could see the masses entering the water five at a time in five-second intervals. Dustin and I gave each other one last high five. With giant naïve smiles on our faces, we slipped on our swim goggles and dove into the water.

The swim was a 2.4-mile course that took you in a triangle pattern. We started on the east side of the Panama City Beach pier. We swam twice its length before turning right at a huge red buoy. From there we swam west to another red buoy. Finally, we turned north and headed back to shore.

Once you reached the shore, you got out of the water and ran back to the east side of the pier to do it all over again. Normally, getting out of the water and getting back in is reprehensible. But this was Ironman, so it didn't bother me one bit.

I walked through some of the small waves as I entered the water. I dove in as we hit the first breakers. The water was cool, but not cold. The waves were small and the current was weak on the first lap.

In most triathlons, especially ocean starts, normalcy consists of mass hysteria. You get kicked in the face many times—and kick others in the face—while you try to claim your spot in the pack. If you are too close to someone when they reach out to take a breath, you inadvertently get dunked. And when someone gets in your lane, you inadvertently dunk them. Honestly, it's *Lord of the Flies: Water Edition*.

Once again, I somehow managed to avoid it all. Part of the reason for this serene start was how they lined athletes up by projected finishing times. The second reason was only five people entered the water at one time, compared to mass starts in the past. As the opening salvo to my first Ironman commenced, I was happy to settle in early and avoid *Wrestle Mania* in the water.

I was surprised how calm I felt for the first section of the swim. My breathing was a little off, but I started slow and let the wetsuit buoyancy do its job. I found myself in a nice clean pocket of water, past the breakers. I even passed a few people on the way. It's hard to explain. You are excited with a rapid heart rate, but calm at the same time. I couldn't believe my mind didn't go straight to the thought of having to do two laps and panic. In the opening 1,000 yards, my mind was blank. I was swimming, not thinking about anything. I was doing what I'd trained my body to do for the past year.

"Just keep swimming. Just keep swimming." Yes, the line from *Finding Nemo* definitely echoed in my head for the first lap of the swim. Dang those little girls!

As I turned the corner at the first buoy, the current helped push me in the right direction. I could feel my speed picking up without extra effort. As I settled in after the turn. I began to recognize my surroundings more and picked up my head to see if I could find Dave or Dustin. This was obviously not going to happen. As far as I could see, everyone looked the same: sleek, black wetsuits and fluorescent swim caps.

I decided to look into the water instead and saw a jellyfish and a small school of silvery fish pass by.

That's when the "thought" kicked in.

Where there are fish, there are bigger fish, and where there are bigger fish there are sharks! Even if there weren't any sharks, the last way I wanted to start off my first Ironman was being stung by a jellyfish! Again, luck was on my side and after that small section and a mini freak-out about sea life, I was cruising.

I reached the shore for the first time, having completed 2,100 yards of swimming, or 1.2 miles. It took me thirty-seven minutes and fifty seconds. Not too bad! I was right at a one minute fifty-eight seconds per one-hundred-yard pace, which is exactly where I wanted to be.

On the beach, the Ironman organizers had set up a water table. It was interesting because in my swim training, I never stopped and drank water. I would put my head down and grind for as long as it took. The ice-cold water at the halfway point of the swim was straight out of *The Waterboy's* magical cooler. Water had never tasted so good in my life, and it gave me a jolt of energy to start lap two.

The second lap was uneventful. I kept my heart rate down. I swam a smooth and steady pace, and I never got out of the little pocket of water with very few people around me. Only for a moment did I think, "Man, this is a long swim. When is this part going to be over?"

I just swam.

Honestly, that was the best part of the entire race. As I exited the water from lap two, my time was one hour, twenty minutes, and fifty-two seconds. An average pace of two minutes and one second per one hundred yards.

I ran up the beach trying to grab the quick release tab on my wetsuit zipper. It is harder than it looks on television. I saw Mike Reilly announcing next to the swim exit sign. It was the first time I had seen him in person. I never got to introduce myself. I wanted to thank him for the signed book that he gave as a gift to Dustin. I knew I didn't have time and neither did he, so I waved to him and yelled, "THANKS, MIKE." As nice as it would have been to have a long conversation with him, I had a race to finish!

# Transition One

The transition area was 500 yards from the swim finish. I got the wetsuit top around my waist and walked to slow my heart rate. Although there were not supposed to be any spectators due to COVID-19 regulations, hordes of people lined the barricades that led into transition. Everyone was cheering and waving, music was playing in the background, and the race was in full swing. Once I found my spot, I was surprised to find Dave still there. His bike was right next to mine on the rack. He looked at me and said, "Nice Swim! I didn't expect to see you yet!" I figured he would have been long gone by then as well. It was a nice surprise.

I sat down, stripped off my wetsuit, threw on my bike jersey, helmet, glasses, and shoes. Then I completed one last mental check. I had four water bottles and six protein bars—one for each hour on the bike—ready to go, along with two peanut butter and jelly sandwiches shoved into the back of my jersey. I clipped into the pedals and off I went.

In my mind, the whole thing happened in less than five minutes. But when I looked back at my time, it actually took me sixteen minutes and fifteen seconds to exit transition one. Time goes by so fast when you are mentally locked-in during a race. Plus, all of my focus was on what was about to happen next. The vaunted, miserable, least favorite discipline, and longest activity of the day. A 112-mile bike ride.

# The Stealth Fighter

I exited through the bike-out inflatable arch and started to pedal. Less than a mile into the course, Kelli, my daughters, Barbara, and all Dustin's family were on the side of the road hooting and hollering like fan girls at a *One Direction* concert. They had homemade signs held up, bright smiling faces, and loud cheering voices to fuel us on the bike. I can't tell you how happy it made me to see them at the beginning of the bike. What a great start to my most dreaded event!

Our team was always there, no matter the time or circumstance. It was like they were racing with us. After passing them we got onto the main road, and I settled in. I leaned into the aero position and set my cadence between eighty-five and ninety revolutions per minute.

Not two miles later, karma from the Chattanooga Waterfront Triathlon came to get me and swung like the hammer of Thor.

It all happened within a five-second window. First, I heard this loud whooshing noise coming from behind me. I thought some fighter jets were flying overhead. There are a few Air Force bases within fifty miles of Panama City. Then the noise got really loud and really close. Next, a flash of black, like a Dementor from *Harry Potter*, came into my peripheral vision and startled me.

I jerked up out of my aerobars.

As I stiffened, a dude doing twenty-five miles per hour on a stealth, jet-black $10,000 bike passed me and was so close that his right pedal hit one of my front-wheel spokes.

I didn't get an "On your left" or even a "Watch out!" This dude literally just blew by me and nicked my front wheel. Before I knew it, he was gone, and I was skidding to a stop on the pavement underneath my $600 bike.

I unclipped my inside shoe that was still attached to the pedal. I cursed something that I will not repeat here and stood up. I checked out my bike to look for any major damage. All I could find was the chain off the crank. I checked my body for damage and found some pretty gnarly road rash on my left calf, upper left forearm, and left shoulder.

Honestly, I was so damn mad at this point that I didn't care about my "scrapes." About that time, Dave passed me on the bike, slowed down, and asked if I was okay. I waved him off and said, "I'm fine! See you in a few hours!" He continued and I hopped back on my bike.

Now let's think about this for one quick second. I had a major bike crash on mile two of a 112-mile bike ride. Mile two! I told my wife before the race, the one thing I was most worried about was the bike. This is because the bike is the one discipline where equipment failure can completely put you out of the race. Not your legs cramping or your lungs about to burst. Your actual equipment could be the end of all your dreams and desires.

If your swim goggles break, you throw them away and squint through it. If your running shoes break, you lose them and run bare foot. You could be on mile one hundred of the race and your bike break. At that point you're done. Forget the year of training and all the time you could have been with your family. All for naught!

This was not going to happen to me. No way in hell!

# One Hundred and Nine Miles of Misery

I pushed off the curb, clipped in, and started pedaling. That's when I heard it for the first time. CHIRP, CHIRP, CHIRP! I started looking around searching for the birds that were tormenting me from overhead, but as I did, I found everyone staring at me. People were passing me on the left and craning their necks around with perplexed looks on their faces.

CHIRP, CHIRP, CHIRP!

I looked down at my front wheel and . . . crap! Maybe this race was going to be over at mile three of the bike. On every revolution of my front tire, it chirped. I also noticed there was a considerable wobble or bend in the tire one second before said CHIRP. On top of that, it was harder to pedal than I remembered in training, and I couldn't gather any momentum. My tire was rubbing on the brake with every revolution and slowing down.

It completely took the wind out of my sails, and the motivation from my body.

When I was wrestling in college, I never fully committed to the sport. I was burnt out from doing it year-round in middle school and high school. The guys I wrestled in college were better than me, and I lost the desire to compete. I specifically remember one tournament at the University of Oklahoma. My dad drove up to watch me for the first time since high school. I proceeded to get beat by a high school senior who entered as an unaffiliated wrestler in the open tournament format. As I walked off the mat, I found a dark corner in the gym and cried my eyes out.

I didn't know why I was still wrestling. I was barely passing my academic classes and struggling to handle the military responsibilities of the Air Force Academy. It wasn't worth it anymore.

My dad tracked me down and we had a long conversation.

He told me, "If you give up or quit, you will never forgive yourself. Wrestling is what got you into the Academy in the first place and if you drop it now, you'll look back in twenty years and always wonder, what if. Even if you never win another match in the next two years, you will have grinded it out. No one can ever say that you gave up."

That conversation immediately entered my brain as the bike and I chirped along at mile three. I credit my mom and dad for how they taught me to always try my hardest and fight through adversity.

I knew I wasn't the most gifted athlete in the world, but I was raised to know that no one was going to outwork me. No one would have the same mental toughness required to accomplish difficult tasks. This is a lesson I instill in my kids every day. I don't know if it gets through to them yet, but I'm hoping they pick up on it as they grow into young adults.

Back to the bike. It's mile fifteen and the bike has been screaming at me for a solid hour. I've been reaching down trying to adjust my brake caliper on the fly. I've inspected every inch of the front tire and tried to figure out how to fix the dang thing.

I finally reached the first bike aid station, dismounted, and fiddled with the tire. I stuck the wheel between my legs and tried to manually bend the tire back straight. I ripped the metal wire from my front brake caliper and opened it up completely.

Then, just to make sure I was completely miserable, I grabbed several alcohol swabs and rubbed hard into the wounds on the left side of my body. I was so pissed off at this point, I didn't feel any pain or discomfort, just pure rage at my current circumstance.

I cleared my mind, gathered up some much-needed courage, ate a protein bar, and filled my water bottles. Back on the bike, I was off again. Miraculously, the chirping went away. The tire was still rubbing and my momentum was null, but I could continue.

Fast forward to mile fifty-six, halfway through the bike course, three hours and forty-nine minutes later. I am flat out miserable!

I'm behind on hydration, I'm biking at fourteen miles an hour instead of the seventeen miles per hour I was expecting, and these damn melted chocolate protein bars are about to send me over the edge! I'm full, but I know I have to keep eating and drinking. As I fumble my way through unwrapping the next protein bar, all the melted chocolate was sticking to my hands and face.

I'm choking it down, not looking up at what's going on around me, when all of the sudden an Ironman Now motorbike pulls up next to me with this super cute girl on the back with her camera.

What a sight I must've been. I'm sure I looked like a five-year-old kid who had a candy bar but was mad because mommy had given me a Snickers instead of Reese's. I had chocolate smeared all over my face. I was sweating like I had just spent a week in the desert and was frowning like the Grinch on Christmas Eve.

I seriously cannot put into words how miserable I was.

The girl raised the camera to take a picture, then paused with the camera just below her eye. I could only imagine what was going through her mind.

Here is this tubby, forty-year-old dude, who looks like he's been thrown in the pit of hell with chocolate covering half of his face, and she's about to take the cover photo for Ironman Florida magazine.

I held up my hand as quick as I could and said, "Oh God, please do not take a picture of me right now!" I let out a pathetic laugh, and she dropped the camera and gave me a thumbs up. "Keep going, you're doing great!" she said.

Even though it was a nice gesture, all I could think was "Please, leave me alone!" Wouldn't you know it, right after I had that thought, it happened again.

CHIRP! CHIRP! CHIRP!

I am now on the verge of insanity. I am about to have a psychotic breakdown. If my tire didn't stop squeaking or if I had to eat one more protein bar, someone was going to get hurt! Luckily, the next aid station was only an hour away, and one of the volunteers was about to change the race for me.

At mile seventy-eight, I pulled over to the side and inspected my bike once more. I realized my tire was not just rubbing the brake, but on the down fork itself. It was so warped at this point, I thought there was no way I could continue. I yelled out to anyone that was listening, "Does anyone have a set of wrenches?" One lone volunteer about twenty feet away yells, "YEAH! HOLD ON!"

He breaks off into a mad sprint away from me and less than two minutes later, he shows up with a wrench set. I use the tool to completely remove my front brake. I undo the quick release on my front tire and raise the fork up off the tire about a quarter inch.

On the front fork of your bike, there are two little notches that sit on top of your wheel axle. The quick release screw tightens everything together. After thinking for the last fifty miles or so, I realized that I might be able to slightly lift the forks off the axle just enough to stop the rubbing, but still keep everything attached. I knew I was risking my front wheel literally rolling off by itself, but that was a risk I was willing to take.

I wasn't going to ride any longer with the chirping noise.

The volunteer held my bike upright the entire time I was working on it. He was sent from heaven above and in just the nick of time.

I was finally riding with no chirping and no rubbing to stop my momentum. That is until I went over a railroad track at mile 106. My fork slid all the way down onto the axle again, and the chirping started back.

With only six miles left I didn't care! Soon I would finally get off this torture device. I promised myself right then and there that I was never going to bike again!

Right before transition two my family was on the side of the road. Their cheering and smiles motivated me, along with the fact that I was almost done. Seven hours, nineteen minutes and forty-nine seconds later, I finished the bike, broken front wheel and all. I wouldn't be surprised if there's a special place in hell where the worst people on the planet are banished to sit on a seat the size of a banana, with a broken front wheel, pedaling endlessly against the brake with a constant chirping sound.

I'm surprised *Dante's Inferno* didn't include it in his tour.

Good thing is, like Dante, I escaped.

Only a marathon left and I could be called an Ironman. What could go wrong?

# Transition Two

I was so happy to get off the bike, I couldn't stand it. I threw the thing back onto the rack and stripped off my bike jersey, shoes, and socks. I threw the queen-sized bedsheet over my head and stripped completely naked. I changed into some comfortable shorts and a cotton T-shirt (the NASA one). This was the most relieving moment of the race, to finally get out of spandex and into something normal. But I have to say, the bedsheet was HOT! It worked well to cover up, but it was like a sauna. I emerged from the sheet and threw on new socks and shoes. I drank a huge bottle of now hot water and blasted onto the run course. Two events down, one to go!

# The Guardian Angel

You would have thought I had learned from previous races, not to go out fast on the run. I didn't. I ran the first mile at an eight-and-a-half-minute per mile pace. Let's say that lasted one whole mile! I was so excited to get off the bike, I couldn't help it. Outside the transition area, spectators lined the barricades and music was blaring. My wife and kids were on the corner screaming motivation my way. It's funny how your body and brain react when you're being watched. No matter how bad things hurt, you never want to look as bad as you feel. You never show weakness as you pass by loved ones in a race. It's the reason everyone who hits the red carpet of an Ironman looks like they just started the race. None of them feel as great as the smiles you see on their faces suggest.

The run course was extremely flat. It turned eastward down Thomas Drive, which is the famous beachside road in Panama City. Along the way, spectators had tents set up, music playing, and giant signs laid out as far as you could see. I remember this one group of really funny women who had on Wonder Woman and Saint Patrick's Day cosplay outfits. When I passed them, they slapped me on the backside and cheered loudly. When I passed them a third time, four hours later, their cheering was significantly enhanced. Their cheers were more slurred, and their slaps were too hard. At least they were steadfast in their support! I applaud all the volunteers and fans. Although some were inebriated, they made the race fun. Even when I was feeling like absolute crap, I mustered up enough energy to say "thank you." It was the least I could do.

Speaking of feeling like crap. Before I hit the 6.1-mile point, something unexpected happened. I had just stopped jogging and was walking to take a break. My face was beet red, I was sweating profusely again, and my lungs felt like they were trying to break out of my rib cage. My heart rate was above 175 beats per minute, and my legs ached.

As I slowed to a crawl, this random dude pops up right next to me and says, "Hey, what's up? You doing alright?"

At this point, I didn't have enough energy to answer, but something about this guy's jovial spirit forced me to oblige.

I told him I felt like crap and my heart rate was getting too high.

He said, "Man, I'm having the same issues…I'll tell you what. You and I are going to finish this Ironman together. We're gonna motivate each other, keep each other company, and make sure that we both get to the finish line! You good with that?"

I said, "Sure, let's do it! But if you find yourself wanting to go on ahead, feel free. I'm not sure how long this is going to take me."

My guardian angel and I got back on the course running side by side. Derick lived in Florida, owned a business, and had kids. His brother was at the race with him, cheering him on. I got to meet the brother and a few friends briefly before the first turnaround. Derick was in my age bracket, and this was his first attempt at an Ironman as well. We ran together. We bitched about pain together. We stopped to eat snacks and get water together. When I needed to walk, he walked with me. When he felt like crap, I stopped with him. We became best friends in a matter of three or four miles.

In that timeframe, we learned each other's life story. I felt like I had known him my entire life. Nothing brings people together like significant events. Moments of glory or pure terror increase that sense of togetherness. We athletes crave shared experiences and support when things get hard.

As I get older, I tend to close myself off to new people and things. It's a natural progression of life. We get old, stubborn, and stuck in our ways. We lose patience and judge people's actions and words. It's kind of sad. I try hard to catch myself when I see this happening.

Luckily for me, Derick didn't give a crap about my grumpy old feelings!

He was going to run with me no matter what.

As we returned to the halfway point, approaching mile thirteen, the sun had completely set. The Panama City Beach fluorescent lights lit up the sky. Hotel towers reached high into the dark night. As we reached the turnaround cone, my wife and kids, along with Dustin's family and Barbara, were waiting for us.

My wife was screaming at the top of her lungs. She sounded like a mental patient released on a day pass from the nut house in *One Flew Over the Cuckoo's Nest*!

At first, I thought she was mad at me. Later, I realized that the Ironman tracker app had stopped updating, like Dave's had on his Lake Placid race. She thought I had dropped out.

Never mind the fact that I told her I hoped to run eleven-minute miles and I was pushing fourteen-minute miles. She was about to start walking down the course to come find me. Low and behold, here came Derick and I with half of the run completed. She said, "GOOOOO! GO! I AM SO PROUD OF YOU! You only have one more loop!"

I turned the corner and ran into the halfway-bag section. I sat on the curb and swapped out my socks and T-shirt. Derick was right there with me. He looked at me and said, "Dude, that was the coolest thing I've ever seen! Your wife just gave me chills. I'm ready to push through this now. What an awesome family."

He was right. I do have an awesome family. They had been awake since 6 a.m., running this race right with me the entire time. They didn't tire, they didn't give up, the thought never even crossed their minds. I realized they were more stressed about the race than we were. They rarely got to see us, and when they did, I'm sure we looked horrible. Their only connection to us during the race was a tracker app and a few transition points. Regardless, they hung in there and when they had the chance, they cheered us on like heroes.

I lifted off the curb, stumbled, then rolled back to the ground. The few minutes sitting down to put on new socks and a new shirt had put me into paralysis. I laughed and Derick did too as I wallowed on the street for a few seconds like a turtle on its back. He grabbed my hand and helped me up. We started the final out-and-back.

# The Finish Line

The last half of the marathon was the hardest thing I've ever done in my entire life. I am not joking. I've done a lot of hard things. I've finished four-hour wrestling practices. I've completed Air Force pilot training and enhanced military survival and resistance training. None of those things compared to the mental challenge that laid ahead of me. They did prepare me though.

My body was an avatar at this point. I couldn't feel a thing. It was an out-of-body experience. Like I said earlier, I've never had a major injury or died and come back to life. But around mile sixteen, I was wishing I was dead. To make matters worse, hundreds of golf carts and monster trucks were on Thomas Drive. They were honking their horns and blaring loud music. This would have been motivating in any other race, but for this point in this race, it just annoyed me. I was barely hanging on to consciousness, trying to put one foot in front of the other. Derick and I started complaining and thinking up creative ways to get back at the crazies cheering us on. Mainly, we just complained because our ideas for revenge didn't make any sense.

Looking back on it now, the mood swings Derick and I went through rivaled a teenager. I remember at the twenty-mile turnaround, there was a group of people with ten-foot PVC poles. On the end of those poles were plastic clapper hands. As you ran by, the people would reach out and "clap" your backside. Derick looked at me and said, "If one of those people catch me just right, I might fall over and quit this race!" I laughed for the first time since mile six. Luckily, we avoided the dreaded clapping plastic hands.

Having turned the corner with only six miles left, our motivation was up as much as could be expected. We were so close, yet so far away from the finish.

We were still having to walk a lot but ended up creating a system to get us through it. We would pick out a streetlight or a walking bridge that went over the highway in the distance and run to it. More like jog to it, but you know what I mean. Once we hit that landmark, we would walk again until we found another spot off in the distance. Once our heart rates slowed and we felt like speeding up, we would run. We did this until finally arriving at one mile to go.

In the distance, there was a bright glow beyond the outdoor mall. The lights were not yellow like streetlamps, they were brighter and more defined. The road seemed to soften for the first time in twenty miles. I miraculously didn't feel like crap anymore.

I felt energy coursing through my body again. All the chest, leg, back, and kidney pain mysteriously disappeared.

I had a new sense of inspired numbness.

Derick and I turned the corner and off in the distance, the music started amplifying. With each step the lights grew brighter. The screams from the crowd grew louder, and the music thumped inside our chests.

We entered the narrow metal barrier chute that led to the finish line. There stood our families. Kelli and my girls had looks of admiration that I'll never forget. Kelli had calmed down a bit and was smiling from ear to ear.

She looked at me as we passed by and said, "I love you! I'm so proud of you."

Shortly after that angelic moment, the red carpet hit our feet. I could not believe it. I told Derick to go ahead and finish before me, but he denied my request.

"NO WAY MAN! We ran twenty miles together and you think I'm going to go ahead of you now? Forget it!" he said.

So, we pushed on together. The bright lights were blinding in the dark night sky. The carpet was beautiful and cushioned under my sore feet. I can't quite remember what song was playing, but it was good. I felt like a Hollywood actor walking down the red carpet.

I was only focusing on one thing.

I wanted to hear Mike Reilly's voice.

Twenty feet from the finish line, I heard it!

"Ryan Brewer, Mississippi…YOU ARE AN IRONMAN!"

I had done it! Despite the fears of becoming supper for some ocean creature. Despite the bike crash and broken front wheel. Despite barely surviving the marathon, I had done it! I held my hands up in triumph and gave Derick an awkward high five. In my head, it was super cool like Goose and Maverick in *Top Gun*. In reality, it looked more like two corpses trying to find each other's hand.

It was finally over. I could stop moving after fifteen hours, twenty-eight minutes, and eleven seconds of gut-wrenching, glorious, repetitive, awful, mind-numbing racing.

# What Happens When You Finish?

You might think I should end the story here. I've chronicled the relationships, life lessons, training, and the race in detail. One thing missing from most Ironman stories is the aftermath. The elation you feel after completing one of the hardest endurance tests in the world is something of legend. What your body does after the elation subsides is something of terror.

Right after I crossed the finish line, I let out a huge sigh of relief. I looked to my right and there sat Dave.

Can you believe the old man beat me?

I found out later, he had crossed the finish line one minute before me. After all that talk about running the race for Dave and helping him across the finish line, my father-in-law, almost thirty years my senior, beat my ass in an Ironman!

I was so proud of him that I didn't care. The Padawan was still learning from the Jedi Master.

I was in a deep fog and nonchalantly said, "Hey Dave." Then walked away. I was so tired and sore. I didn't realize his knee was hurting badly, and he was sitting in a wheelchair. My brain was not functioning. I walked past him to get my medal, some food, and my bike.

I was a zombie with no brain, no thoughts, nothing. I've never witnessed anything like it. Dave was just another competitor to me at that point. I didn't have the energy or wherewithal to hug his neck and celebrate with him.

A side note on Dave and his knee: The night before the race, Barbara pulled Dave aside for a pep talk of sorts. She had seen the almost finish at Ironman Lake Placid. She had lived the collapse at Kennesaw Mountain and the years of bad pain in his knees.

She told him, "Dave, I love you, but this is your last race. We are not doing this again, so if your knee starts hurting, you keep right on going. We will get you a new knee once you finish."

So, Dave finished . . . ahead of me. Afterwards, he drank beer till 2 a.m. like the champ he is.

I did a death march to the transition area after picking up a post-race food box. It was the longest 300-yard walk of my life. I dropped the box on the ground at least three times because I couldn't concentrate. I was alone, in the dark, still watching people pass by on the course to my left. I had no energy to cheer them on.

I arrived at my bike, then laid down and took a nap! It was more like I passed out, but we'll call it a nap.

There I was, passed out in the transition area, spread eagle on the pavement. I awoke some unknown time later. It dawned on me that I somehow had to get my bike and gear out of the transition area. That's when my wonderful wife came to the rescue.

COVID-19 led to some pretty strict protocols on spectators. No one was allowed in the transition area or the Ironman Village unless they were an athlete.

Those protocols never met my wife.

Her dad was in a wheelchair at the medical tent and her husband was passed out in the transition area, not answering his phone. Needless to say, Kelli told the volunteers that she was going in to get her boys.

After a few protests, she threw out the, "I'm a Nurse" card and said, "I'm going to get my dad and husband!"

The volunteers were smart to let her go, and that's all I'm going to say about that!

Kelli got her dad after she went into the Village and bought everybody hats.

Also not allowed under COVID-19 Protocols!

She wheeled him to transition where she found me laying on the ground like a corpse. The only thing I clearly remember is her asking what I wanted to do with my bike.

I loudly stated, "Throw it in the dumpster, because I'm never riding that thing again!"

We collected our gear and hobbled out of transition where Barbara had pulled up the car.

I haven't mentioned Dustin in a while and there's a reason for that.

Dustin finished the race in twelve hours, twenty-eight minutes, and one second!

After we gave the high five to each other at swim start, I never saw him again. He had already eaten and was asleep at the condo when Dave and I finished the race.

The guy is an animal and a purist. Boy, can he race! One of these days he will qualify for the Kona Ironman World Championship. I hope I can be there to run with him the last 300 yards of the finish line, like he's done for me so many times over the years.

# The Gross Part

This part is a little gross, so if you want to skip the next few paragraphs, I won't blame you. I'm not writing this to deter you from trying an Ironman, but I want you to know the truth and how I learned from it. If it was that bad, do you think I'd be writing this story? Or would I have completed two more triathlons, including a half Ironman since?

My wife led me into the condo, helped me strip, and get into the shower. I could barely lift my hands over my head. The hot water and soap felt amazing, but it stung on the now dried- up scabs from the bike crash. Kelli was in nurse mode.

She knew I was in bad shape and was watching me like a hawk. I rinsed and got out of the shower to dry off.

Afterwards, I tried to pee for the first time in seven hours. As I looked in the toilet, I called out to Kelli. The toilet bowl was full of brown, bloody urine. Being the amazing nurse she is, Kelli calmly helped me dress and put me into bed.

She then proceeded to wake me up every thirty minutes and shove a water bottle into my mouth. She made me drink as much as I possibly could until 4 a.m.

The only way to describe the pain and suffering I was feeling is this. I felt like I was waking up from surgery but also having the worst hangover of my life at the same time.

Kelli told me I made the most horrible groans and noises she had ever heard while I tried to sleep.

I don't remember any of it.

Kelli was pretty sure my kidneys were failing because they were processing too much muscle protein from the race. The medical term is rhabdomyolysis. The protein bars I ate during the bike had 600 calories and 40 grams of protein each. I thought it would be a good idea to mix it up with peanut butter and jelly sandwiches. Let's not forget the tasty pepperoni pizza and Diet Dr. Pepper I had the day before the race as well.

To sum it up, my nutrition was crap and I was an idiot. My body was making me pay and would continue to do so for the next thirty-six hours.

I awoke around 9 a.m. the next day and finally peed again.

It was yellow! Thank GOD!

My wife sighed with relief. Without her care, I might've been in the emergency room. I owe her a life debt for all the help that night. I stumbled around in my pajamas, looking like an eighty-year-old man all day. My eyes were sunken in and you could see all the bones in my face. I started the race at 175 pounds. I weighed 160 pounds the next morning.

My legs would randomly cramp and lock up.

Getting up from the couch was a lot harder than I remembered.

I pumped in water and Gatorade as best I could and relaxed. I couldn't walk upright for the next twenty-four hours. Normalcy started to return thirty-six hours post-race. By the time we checked out of the hotel and started the six-hour drive home, I was starting to feel human again.

The following day, Dustin, Dave, and I hobbled to the parking lot to head home. We looked like three geriatrics hunched over and gingerly walking on hurting legs and knees. Even so, we proudly rolled our bikes by our sides with wristbands and medals still attached.

Dave was finally able to put the Ironman sticker on the back of his SUV. We were tired, but we felt accomplished. We had completed something that very few people could say they've done.

We were all IRONMEN!

# Afterthoughts

Ask anyone who's done an Ironman, "Why did you do it?" They will give you a myriad of answers.

One of the most common answers you will hear is "For the tattoo!"

So shortly after we arrived home, I got mine.

It was my second tattoo ever. If you knew me, you wouldn't think I was the kind of person to have tattoos. I got my first one in college to represent the four years of wrestling at the Air Force Academy.

Here I was, forty years old, getting my second and final tattoo: the famous Ironman red M with a red circle centered at the top, aka The M-Dot. I've always said that when I'm old and my skin is saggy, I better have a pretty good story for the tattoos on my back. I'll enjoy explaining these to my grandkids. Dustin and Dave talked a big game but never saw it through. They might have beaten me in the race, but I'll always have the ink!

Derick, on the other hand, sent me a text a few weeks later showing me his tattoo. I was super proud of him.

Dave had knee surgery after the new year. He is completely healed now, although he will never competitively run again. He still rides the bike daily and plans on finding some other records to break as he continues to never age. I think his next competition will be on an indoor rowing machine. I'm pretty sure he can be the national champion of his age group.

Whenever I go visit Dave and Barbara, we talk about the Great Race. We gawk at the medals and plaques sitting in his basement office. We reminisce on our amazing journey.

Mike Reilly sent me a message the day after the race. He wrote, "Congrats on your fifteen-hour, twenty-eight minute, and eleven second Ironman."

How great was that? The man had been up for nearly twenty-four hours announcing every athlete as they crossed the finish line. He made the effort to look up my time and personally message me. What a class act! Mike is the greatest ambassador of any sport I've ever been a part of. I hope he continues to call races forever. It will be a sad day when he retires and people don't get the chance to hear his voice as they cross the finish line.

Finally, Kelli ended up getting the information on how to order the finisher's frame that I was too superstitious to buy before the race. She gave it to me as a Christmas gift, along with almost everything you can find in the Ironman store.

Dustin and I took several months off but have since raced in two triathlons. We completed a sprint distance triathlon in Tupelo, Mississippi, in March 2021. Dustin won the Masters group with the fastest time for everyone above forty, and I won my age group. Okay, so really, I got second *again* because Dustin won overall, but I slotted up to first in my age group due to his blazing speed.

In May 2021 we both completed Ironman Chattanooga 70.3. Dustin finished in five hours and thirty-six minutes. I finished in six hours and thirty-seven minutes. I had learned a lot about nutrition and hydration from Florida. I also learned how to train correctly. I cut my full Ironman time by more than half, and I didn't feel like a zombie afterwards.

It also didn't hurt that I bought a brand new, fluorescent yellow, Canyon CF 7.0 tri bike with disk brakes and aero wheels! My average bike time went from fourteen miles per hour to 19.14 miles an hour. I am starting to enjoy biking now, just a little!

The old bike that I asked my wife to throw in the dumpster sits on my indoor trainer. I still haven't taken the Ironman stickers off. I hate that bike, but it reminds me of the pain and dedication it takes to finish such a daunting task.

I don't know what's next. I've spent thousands of dollars on gear and races. I've spent countless hours of training, but my diet still sucks.

I do know one thing.

If I go more than seven days without working out, I get cranky.

Completing an Ironman changes you. Working out becomes less of something you do and more of a lifestyle. You feel better when you work out. The endorphin release alone is worth chasing. You also can eat like crap and not get fat. Plus, you get to listen to music while you train.

More than anything, finishing an Ironman is a mental accomplishment. Once you complete one, you have the mindset of "anything is possible," just like their slogan says. Although we talk about all the training and hours of preparation, at some point during an Ironman none of it matters.

The only thing that matters is your mental toughness and your ability to suffer.

The human body is capable of so many amazing things. Sometimes you have to test that ability by trying something impossibly hard. You just might surprise yourself.

I hope my girls will one day understand what I did and why I worked out so much over that year of their life.

Who knows, maybe they will start doing triathlons and want me to train with them, like Dave did for me.

I hope they find out that the hard things in life are worth doing. The amount of pride you feel after completing something like an Ironman stays with you forever. I want them to enjoy that feeling for themselves.

Will I ever do another full Ironman? Hell No!

Well, I'll keep telling myself that for now. But you never know what the future holds. Thanks for taking this journey with me, now get out there and take one yourself.

## Triathlon Races and Times

| | Swim | Transition 1 | Bike | Transition 2 | Run | Overall |
|---|---|---|---|---|---|---|
| Chattanooga Waterfront Tri | 1.5K | | 40K | | 10K | |
| June 23, 2019 | 0:28:08 | 4:15 | 1:26:27 | 3:12 | 1:05:31 | 3:07:35 |
| Possumtown Triathlon | 600 yd | | 17 mi | | 3.3 mi | |
| August 17, 2019 | 13:49 | 2:48 | 0:57:27 | 2:31 | 0:28:27 | 1:45:00 |
| Ironman Florida | 2.4 mi | | 112 mi | | 26.2 mi | |
| November 7, 2020 | 1:20:52 | 16:15 | 7:19:49 | 15:45 | 6:15:32 | 15:28:10 |
| Tupelo Sprint Triathlon | 300 meter | | 11 mi | | 2 mi | |
| April 24, 2021 | 5:37 | 1:21 | 0:57:27 | 1:02 | 15:30 | 0:56:55 |
| Ironman 70.3 Chattanooga | 1.4 mi | | 56 mi | | 13.1 mi | |
| May 23, 2021 | 0:39:04 | 7:43 | 2:58:18 | 6:13 | 2:46:09 | 6:37:24 |
| Heart of Dixie Triathlon | .5 mi | | 27.5 mi | | 7 mi | |
| July 24, 2021 | 16:31 | 1:40 | 1:22:27 | 2:57 | 1:14:29 | 2:58:22 |
| Dragon Fly Triathlon | .5 mi | | 18 mi | | 4 mi | |
| September 21, 2021 | 13:55 | 1:47 | 0:53:33 | 1:32 | 0:41:10 | 1:51:55 |